Closing
the
POVERTY
&Culture Gap

Closing
the
POVERTY
&Culture Gap

**Strategies
to Reach
Every
Student**

Donna Walker Tileston
Sandra K. Darling
Foreword by **Belinda Williams**

CORWIN
A SAGE Company

For information:

Corwin
A SAGE Company
2455 Teller Road
Thousand Oaks, California 91320
(800) 233-9936
Fax: (800) 417-2466
www.corwinpress.com

SAGE Ltd.
1 Oliver's Yard
55 City Road
London EC1Y 1SP
United Kingdom

SAGE India Pvt. Ltd.
B 1/I 1 Mohan Cooperative Industrial Area
Mathura Road, New Delhi 110 044
India

SAGE Asia-Pacific Pte. Ltd.
33 Pekin Street #02-01
Far East Square
Singapore 048763

Printed in the United States of America.

Library of Congress Cataloging-in-Publication Data

Tileston, Donna Walker.
Closing the poverty and culture gap : strategies to reach every student / Donna E. Walker Tileston and Sandra K. Darling.
        p. cm.
Includes bibliographical references and index.
ISBN 978-1-4129-5530-0 (cloth)
ISBN 978-1-4129-5531-7 (pbk.)

    1. Poor children—Education—United States. 2. Children of minorities—Education—United States. 3. Children with social disabilities—Education—United States. 4. Multiculturalism—United States. I. Darling, Sandra K. II. Title.

LC4091.T54 2009
371.826'9420973—dc22   2008049670

This book is printed on acid-free paper.

14 15 16 17 18 10 9 8 7 6 5 4 3

Acquisitions Editor:	Carol Chambers Collins
Editorial Assistant:	Brett Ory
Production Editor:	Cassandra Margaret Seibel
Copy Editor:	Mary L. Tederstrom
Typesetter:	C&M Digitals (P) Ltd.
Proofreader:	Susan Schon
Indexer:	Terri Corry
Cover Designer:	Scott Van Atta

Contents

Foreword

Belinda Williams, PsyD

Cognitive psychologist and editor of
Closing the Achievement Gap: A Vision for Changing Beliefs and Practices

In this book, Tileston and Darling define and elaborate the central role of culture in the development of children living in poverty. They outline the ways in which the cultural dimensions of learning must be central in teaching and learning environments and reforms proposed to close achievement gaps. The book provides an analysis of why federal interventions, Title I and The No Child Left Behind Act (NCLB), and funding, as well as extended day and tutoring approaches have failed. The perspective and knowledge of the critical role of culture in learning invites us to understand what is missing in the attempts of the current system of education and what must be changed in the system to successfully educate millions of students whose cultural/daily experiences do not match the culture of schools as they exist today.

The most important contribution of this volume is the evidence presented to support the rejection of the deficit interpretation of the achievement gaps that exist among groups of disadvantaged and diverse students and their more advantaged peers. An asset model of learning and achievement differences offers educators strategies to adapt instruction without lowering expectations and standards. Definitions of cognition, intrinsic motivation, brain research, and resilience are elaborated and the best ways to provide instruction that integrates these understandings are discussed. Implications for leadership, teacher preparation and professional development are delineated.

Tileston and Darling offer a valuable tool for those committed to providing the best education possible for students the education system has traditionally failed. Those responsible in higher education institutions, government agencies, districts and schools will find the research, knowledge, and strategies synthesized by the authors a refreshing shift for comprehensive planning to ensure the education of all students. As the authors conclude, "the consequences for ignoring the educational differences and needs of [culturally diverse] children of poverty will impact all of us."

Acknowledgments

Corwin gratefully acknowledges the contributions of the following reviewers:

Thomas S. C. Farrell
Professor
Brock University
St. Catharines, Ontario, Canada

Steve Hutton
Area Coordinator
Kentucky Center for Instructional Discipline
Villa Hills, KY

Toby J. Karten
Educator, Author, Adjunct Professor
College of New Jersey, Gratz University, Drew University
Marlboro, NJ

Mary Reeve
Director, Services for Exceptional Students
Gallup McKinley County Schools
Gallup, NM

Bill Sommers
Corwin author
Program Associate, Southwest Educational Development Laboratory
Austin, TX

Rosemary Traoré
Assistant Professor, Urban Education
University of North Carolina at Charlotte
Charlotte, NC

About the Authors

Donna Walker Tileston has served education as a leader in teaching, administration, research, writing, software development, and national consulting for the past 30 years. She has been responsible for curriculum development, management, technology, finance, grants management, public relations, and drug abuse prevention programs. For the past 25 years she has been actively involved in brain research, including factors that inhibit learning or increase the brain's ability to put information into long-term memory. Tileston's 10-book collection *What Every Teacher Should Know* (Corwin, 2003) received the 2004 Distinguished Achievement Award for Excellence in Educational Publishing by the American Educational Publishers Association. Other Corwin titles include *Strategies for Active Learning* (2006); *What Every Parent Should Know About Schools, Standards, and High-Stakes Tests* (2005); *Training Manual for What Every Teacher Should Know* (2005); *Ten Best Teaching Practices: How Brain Research, Learning Styles, and Standards Define Teaching Competencies* (2005); and *Strategies for Teaching Differently: On the Block or Not* (1998). Tileston has presented extensively at local, state, national, and international conferences, including in The Hague in November 2005 and in Warsaw during March 2006.

Sandra K. Darling is the founder and president of Learning Bridges. Grounded in five years of research, the Learning Bridges Aligned Instructional Database contains the most effective, research-based instructional strategies for the standards of all states—in rank order of their power to impact learning. Born into extreme poverty in rural Minnesota, Dr. Darling understands the power of having significant adults in her life who believed in her, held high expectations for her, and taught her the value of integrity. She received her bachelor's degree, three master's degrees, and a PhD from the University of Minnesota in related areas of education. She has coauthored three books in education and published articles in several education journals. She has presented to thousands of educators on standards-based education, curriculum alignment, inclusion practices, transformational leadership, school improvement, strategic planning, and assessment practices. She is the leading expert on aligning instructional strategies to content standards and delivering that instruction with the modifications to close the gap in achievement for diverse learners, that is, students from poverty, those from diverse cultures, and English language learners.

Introduction

In some respects, the conditions of poverty and near-poverty are worse than the statistics would indicate. The reason for this is that several key social and public goods have become increasingly inaccessible for a number of American households. In particular, a quality education, health care, affordable housing, and child care either are out of reach or are obtained only at the cost of considerable economic expenditure and hardship. Yet these social goods are vital in building and maintaining healthy and productive citizens and families.

—Mark R. Rank, *One Nation, Underprivileged*

According to researchers such as Rank (2005), we have lived under the deficit model for viewing poverty for some time. The assumption has often been that since the economic system generates prosperity for anyone willing to work hard, if you are poor it must mean that you are a personal failure. After all, this is the land of opportunity. Living in poverty means that you failed to work hard or that you have a lack of intelligence or some other character flaw. Rank points to the research of Gilder (1981), Hernstein and Murray (1994), and Schwartz (2000) who list the common assumptions about why people are poor:

1. Absence of strong morals

2. Failure to exert responsibility

3. Laziness

4. An inability to save for the future

5. Lack of intelligence

6. Addictions to alcohol or drugs

In other words, we often view poverty through the lens of inadequacy, and indeed many of our "solutions" for closing achievement gaps in school hover around a plan to "fix" poor kids. Many of these plans have involved special pull-out programs, retention, and a temptation to make sweeping assumptions about children from poverty that would have us assume that all children from poverty are alike. After years and hundreds of millions of dollars spent on programs to close the gap, we now know that there is something at work here besides just poverty. We also know that all children from poverty are not alike.

In this book we examine the effects of poverty on children, but we will not make the assumption that all poverty is alike. Indeed, there is a vast difference between the effects of poverty on children living in a volatile inner-city neighborhood riddled with daily violence and a child living in poverty in rural America. These are cultural differences, and they do not stop with this example; culture is the lens through which we view the world, and it affects how we approach education. Culture is created by heritage and by environment, by the approach to learning and by how it is valued. Culture includes the expectations, traditions, values, roles, and modes of learning that may go back thousands of years. Culture is reinforced daily in the home and in the neighborhood, and the culture of the home is sometimes in direct contradiction to the culture of the classroom, and vice versa.

The culture of a Native American child living on a reservation is different from that of a Mexican American child living in South Texas with parents who are migrant workers. They both live in poverty, but their approach to education, the way in which they view authority, and how they view school may be very different because of their culture.

Culture has such a strong influence on children and how they learn that we recommend teachers look at culture first and then poverty as they modify best practices to meet these needs. We also recommend that educators view culture from the standpoint that these children may have had different experiences than their middle-class counterparts and that we need to build on and expand the positive experiences rather than trying to change them.

For more than two decades, education has struggled with how to make education equitable to a population that has changed dramatically in that time. In the last century, education seemed to get it right for those children who were middle or upper class and who came from an Anglo-Saxon culture. Test scores and other data bear this out. However, educators and the system of education in general are in turmoil over how to teach to cultures that do not fit the middle-class, Anglo-Saxon background. Teachers are leaving the field in droves, not because they do not know their subject matter but because they do not know how to teach their students effectively. For many teachers, self-efficacy has eluded them, and coming to school each day to face failure is not appealing. When offered more money to teach in high-poverty areas, many teachers opt out because it is often frustrating and time consuming trying to reach a population that is not responding positively. Principals and other instructional leaders are often overwhelmed by the issues facing them and feel powerless to help teachers to be successful.

It is not that principals, teachers, and other members of the education system do not care or are not aware—nothing could be further from the truth. We often say that if someone told us that students would be more successful if we learned to stand on our heads, we would give it a try. Teachers and administrators are passionate about wanting students to be successful. They are growing weary of being told they need to get test scores up, dropout rates down, and graduation rates up; educators are ready for someone to tell them how and to have the research to back it up.

In the last century, education experimented with many new ideas in working with all children. From differentiation to models on poverty, we tried many new ideas, and though we made some progress, gaps remained. We now know from the research on past experiences that there is not a "one size fits all" approach to working with children from poverty. We know that, while poverty makes a marked difference in achievement without appropriate intervention, just differentiating for poverty alone is not enough. If we are to provide instructional practices that make a difference in student learning, we must address culture first, poverty second.

It is our purpose in this book to provide a framework for teaching that includes the instructional practices that make the most difference in student learning modified for culture *and* poverty, not just for poverty. We have based this book not on observations, but on research about what makes the most difference in learning, research on the brain and learning, and research on how various cultures approach learning.

In Chapter 1 we examine some of the more common models for dealing with gaps in learning in schools today. Next, we introduce the reader to the reasons why culture matters so much and why recognizing this is essential to any model if we are truly going to make a difference in closing the gaps. The reader is introduced to a six-part framework that is the underpinning of this book. This framework addresses key structures that must be in place to effectively work with culture and poverty.

In Chapter 2 we discuss motivation and why many cultures in our schools are "turned off" by our typical approach. We examine brain research on how motivation is turned on in the brain and ways that we can modify our approaches in the classroom to tap into how the students in our classrooms are motivated to learn from within. Only *you* can motivate you—and the same is true of your students: all motivation comes from within. That is the bad news; the good news is that we can lead our students to the natural motivation with which they are born by addressing some of the issues that affect the brain's desire to learn; for example, making the classroom instruction culturally relevant helps to tap into the motivation of the diverse classroom.

Chapter 3 is a discussion of how we build resilience in our students by using research-based and culturally appropriate practices in the classroom. Resiliency—the ability to survive and thrive in the face of difficult circumstances—is the characteristic that will lift our students out of poverty, and it is resiliency that will keep them in school even when circumstances are difficult. The ultimate goal of everything that we discuss in this book is to build this resiliency. Turnaround teachers are educators that have the ability to build resiliency in their students.

Chapter 4 introduces the cognitive system and discusses how best to provide instruction to students. In this chapter we discuss declarative learning, which makes up most of the learning in the classroom. Declarative information requires the appropriate storage in the brain so that it can be retrieved on those days it is needed. Unfortunately, most declarative learning is taught through lecture and is stored in the semantic pathway, which is the least reliable for retrieval. Add to that the fact that this pathway requires the learner to have the vocabulary skills for appropriate retrieval. Students from poverty often start school with as little as half the vocabulary of their middle-class counterparts, and students from other cultures may have even less exposure to the vocabulary of the classroom. It is no wonder that these students struggle in the typical classroom that relies so heavily on verbal skills.

Chapter 5 explores the second area of the cognitive system—procedural learning. This is the most difficult part of learning because it requires the students to do something with the declarative information. Students must have an understanding of the factual information (declarative) in order to demonstrate that they can use it in some way (procedural knowledge). They must demonstrate not only that they can use the declarative information but also that they can use it appropriately. For example, students learning about estimation must be able to use that information in a real-world context, not just in that of the classroom. Indeed, many of the states' standards and benchmarks specifically declare that students must be able to demonstrate understanding in a real-world setting.

Chapter 6 is a discussion of the task of the instructional leader in the school as he or she gathers the resources needed to address all of the needs of children from poverty. It is a call to all educators to join hands with the social, emotional, spiritual, physical, and educational resources of communities so that we can lift students from poverty. Poverty is not just a problem for the police force or for the housing authority; it is a problem for all of us because it is robbing us of resources in terms of productive citizens and tax dollars.

In Chapter 7 we merge all of the information from the chapters to examine this new framework and create strategies to use it in your school.

A decade ago, Dr. Belinda Williams edited a book called *Closing the Achievement Gap*. Very few of the ideas and suggestions of that book have been brought to fruition today—and yet the problems of a decade ago remain. The time has come to demand the resources, the research, and the training to lead students of poverty to daily success. It is time as well to provide teachers with instructional practices that really do make a difference in acknowledging culture and poverty in education. We must create the middle class of the future by providing the scaffolding that builds resiliency in our students of poverty. We hope the discussions in this book will be a beginning for you and for those you teach.

Culture and Poverty 1

Caring teachers everywhere are working harder to improve student achievement—attending more meetings, analyzing more data, testing students more often, focusing on more scripted curriculum, responding to pacing guides, encouraging students to stay in school—and yet they tell us that they continue to be overwhelmed and frustrated, especially in low-performing, high-poverty schools. Whether they teach six-year-olds or sixteen-year-olds, teachers recognize that there are students whose needs they are supposed to meet but for whom none of the strategies they know work. Teachers are pressured to "accept the responsibility" for every student's learning, with the accompanying rewards for success and punishments for failure. Given the extent of teachers' efforts, why do the problems of low achievement persist for some children? Why are there still gaps in achievement between groups of students?

This chapter will (a) identify the achievement gaps based on culture and poverty, (b) review the approaches that education has used in the past to address the achievement gaps for students living in poverty and for students from diverse cultures, (c) identify what is missing from these approaches, and (d) identify the research-based components of a new approach that will meet the needs of the millions of students who are falling through the cracks of an educational system that has been extremely successful in improving achievement for white, middle-class children.

What Is the Achievement Gap for Culture and Poverty?

Sometimes it helps to "see" the issues that we are attempting to address. To provide you with a visual representation of the concern, Figure 1.1 shows the results of California's state test results from 2006.

The graph is from Closing the Achievement Gap: Report of Superintendent Jack O'Connell's California P–16 Council (2008, p. 3). In California, an Academic Performance Index (API) score of 800 is considered an acceptable level of performance, and it is the goal of most schools. According to the information in Figure 1.1, children for all grades achieve an API score of 801—acceptable achievement. African American students for all grades score 166 points below that of white children. American Indian students for all grades score 110 points below that of white children. Hispanic/Latino students for all grades score 145 points below that of white children. Pacific Islander children for all grades score 87 points below that of white children. Only children of Filipino and Asian ancestry score above white children. Economically disadvantaged children score 33 percentile points below white children in language arts and 23 percentile points below white children in mathematics (California Standardized Testing and Reporting [STAR] Program; P-16 Council, 2008, p. 3). According to the P-16 Council, "California's educational system suffers from a racial/ethnic achievement gap that causes students of color to be *consistently outperformed by their white peers even when controlling for poverty*" (p. 17, emphasis in original). This means that children from diverse cultures who are *not* poor are performing below their white classmates who are poor.

Lest we believe the issues are limited to California, let's look at the other side of the United States, at North Carolina. Figure 1.2 represents a picture of North Carolina's fourth graders.

Based on the 2007 National Assessment of Educational Progress (NAEP) data, African American, Hispanic, and American Indian children are scoring 21 to 27 points below white children in achievement. As reported in California,

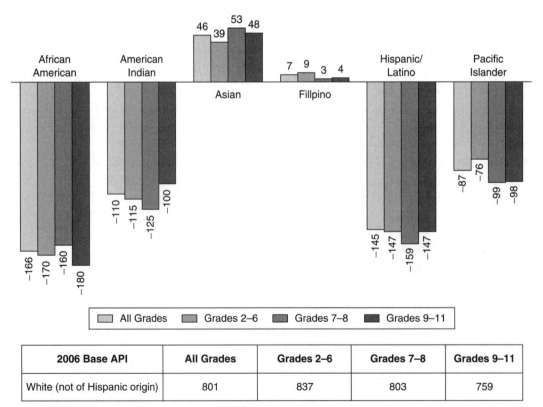

2006 Base API	All Grades	Grades 2–6	Grades 7–8	Grades 9–11
White (not of Hispanic origin)	801	837	803	759

Base: 2006 Academic Performance Index (API) for White Students

Figure 1.1   California Achievement Gap by Race

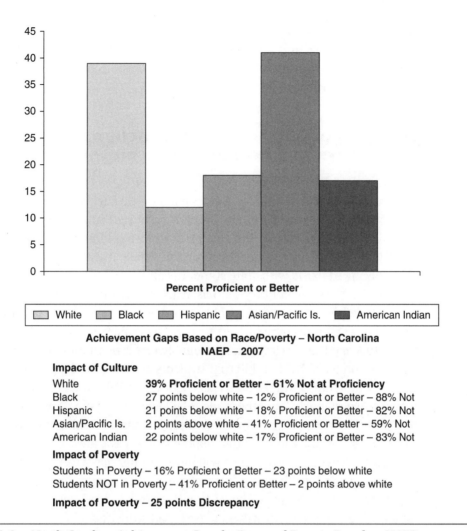

Figure 1.2   North Carolina Achievement Gaps for Race and Poverty Based on NAEP

SOURCE: Darling, 2008

Asian/Pacific Islander children score above their white classmates. Students living in poverty score 23 points below white children. Middle-class or affluent students score *slightly above* their classmates who live in poverty. The difference in achievement based on poverty is 25 points.

Whether we examine state tests or national tests, the results are consistent. There exists a gap in achievement between white students and students from diverse cultures. There exists a gap in achievement between middle-class and affluent students and students living in poverty. Therefore, educators who are interested in improving academic achievement must address the issues of culture and poverty in order to accomplish that goal.

What Models/Approaches Have Been Tried

As we have learned over the last decade, there is no simple, one-size-fits-all solution to the issues around closing the gaps in achievement. Various programs such as compensatory education, Title I, English as a second language, various pull-out programs, and a range of other initiatives have left us with the same gaps and a great deal of frustration. Why have we failed so miserably with these well-meaning programs?

Focusing on Curriculum, Instruction, and Assessment to Improve Achievement

In the last decade, achievement improvement efforts have strongly focused on curriculum, instruction, and assessment—the key processes in education. Districts that have the fiscal and human resources have spent thousands of hours making sure that their district curriculum is aligned to state standards. Districts without those resources depend on the textbook publishers to ensure that alignment exists with state standards and view the textbook as their curriculum. In many elementary schools, teachers are mandated to cover curriculum detailed by pacing guides that prescribe what should be taught on any given day. The intent here is to ensure that all children are provided an opportunity to learn the curriculum, presumably resulting in increased student performance on tests. Never mind that students do not have the prerequisite skills for learning what is taught on a specific day. The thinking is that the curriculum will "spiral back," and the student will learn it the next time. The theory is that if students don't learn the curriculum to mastery—meaning well enough to retain the learning and to build upon it (Guskey & Gates, 1986; Kulik, Kulik, & Bangert-Drowns, 1990)—they will have another opportunity to learn it. The focus here is on teaching, not learning, and certainly not on the learner. This approach is grounded in the belief that if we focus clearly on the expectations for learning, achievement will increase for all students.

Another focus for improving achievement for all children is increasing assessment. Districts and states in which we have worked have examined summative, end-of-class or end-of-grade assessments; formative, benchmark assessments; textbooks assessments; teacher-made classroom assessments; performance-based assessments; and a host of other ways to find out if students are learning what they are expected to learn. More and more time is spent on assessment—both the teacher's time and the students' time. Most assessments focus on measuring whether or not students have grasped the information, or declarative knowledge, of the curriculum being taught. We know that 80–90% of what state assessments measure is the vocabulary and concepts of the state standards (Marzano, Kendall, & Gaddy, 1999). Vocabulary and concepts are declarative knowledge. Very little assessment is performed on procedural knowledge—what students should be able to demonstrate or do—measuring whether the student can apply or use that information in a real-life situation. The reasons for this are that skills and processes are difficult to assess and performance assessments are very time consuming to administer and score accurately, are expensive, and require more class time.

The focus on assessment to improve achievement is grounded in the belief that having assessment data will focus improvement efforts and will inform instruction (Tomlinson, 2008). Rarely does that happen in real life. Guskey

(2008) states, "Assessments alone do little to improve student learning or teaching quality. What really counts is what happens *after* the assessments. Just as regularly checking your blood pressure does little to improve your health if you do nothing with the information gained, what matters most with formative assessments is how students and teachers use the results. Unfortunately, many educators today overlook this vital aspect of formative assessment" (p. 28). Principals and teachers get assessment results. Principals, whose job it is to focus school improvement efforts on achievement, tell us they examine assessment results but are not sure which school improvement solutions at their disposal will make a difference in achievement. Teachers, whose job it is to focus on instruction, do not know which instructional strategies will make a difference in achievement for the low scores reported on assessment results for their students.

Teachers know different instructional strategies (the more experienced a teacher, the more strategies he or she knows), but most teachers are unaware of which instructional strategies work best (or have the greatest impact on student achievement) for specific grade-level standards. Although research-based instructional strategies have been aligned to grade-level standards in all states for two content areas (Darling, 1999), that information is not widely known. In addition, teachers that we work with tell us that they are unsure what to do differently for their students of poverty and from diverse cultures. On the bright side, schools are beginning to engage their teachers in learning communities. One of the ways for teachers to change what happens in classrooms is to meet regularly to focus on instructional practice.

Both principals and teachers know that something *must* happen in the classroom between teachers and students to make a difference in learning. Wenglinsky (2002) measured the impact of effective classroom practice on achievement. His results indicate that the highest predictor of academic achievement is the proficiency of teachers on effective instructional practice. When combined with professional development on effective instruction (ES = .98), teachers have the power to override poverty (ES = .76).

What do these measures mean? An effect size (shown as ES) is a statistical measure of the impact on achievement of a "treatment" (in this case, effective instructional practice, professional development on effective practice, and poverty). Effect size is a measure designed to quantify the effectiveness of a specific intervention as compared with another intervention. Effect sizes between .2 and .5 are generally considered small, those between .5 and .8 are considered medium, and those .8 and greater are considered large. Effect size is a significant measure because it can be translated into percentile points gained or lost in achievement. An ES of .98 for professional development means that it will impact academic achievement by .98 (of 1.0) standard deviation, which equates to 34 percentile points. If student achievement was at the 50th percentile *without* the professional development on effective instruction, the "treatment" of incorporating professional development would increase achievement 34 points (to the 84th percentile)—a significant impact on learning.

Which instructional strategies make the most difference in learning (have the highest ES) for their curriculum is not known by most teachers. Generally, they use those strategies that they know how to deliver in the classroom. In later chapters, we provide effective instructional strategies for the two categories of knowledge that are represented by curriculum and state standards. We have selected those strategies that, when delivered appropriately, will make a difference in learning for students of poverty as well as those from diverse cultures.

Deficit Thinking Does Not Work

There have been approaches proposed that are grounded in a deficit model of thinking. These approaches start from the assumption that students of poverty and diverse cultures have deficits that teachers need to "fix" to improve achievement. Teachers are provided with lists of deficit characteristics that their students bring to school, for example, poor vocabulary, lack of background knowledge, being unmotivated, being inattentive, dysfunctional families, being involved with gangs and drugs, refusal to complete assignments (and sometimes refusal to even start them), and the list goes on. Programs have evolved that are intended to increase the awareness of these characteristics, grounded in classroom observations of students living in poverty and from diverse cultures. There is rarely a mention of the assets that these students bring to the learning experience. Most of the deficit programs are not supported by research.

The most prominent approach that represents "a classic example of what has been identified as deficit thinking" (Bomer, Dworin, May, & Simington, 2007) is that of Ruby Payne's teacher education program, *A Framework for Understanding Poverty* (Payne, 2005). The authors Bomer and colleagues examined the professional development based on Payne's program in order to analyze the relationship between Payne's claims and the existing research about low-income individuals and families. Though this was the first study to explore the content basis of Payne's inservice teacher education program, the authors reported that "others who have reviewed the book have been in accord with our analysis" (Gorski, 2006; Ng & Rury, 2006; Osei-Kofi, 2005). Their research centered on two research questions: What patterns are detectable in Payne's truth claims about children's lives in poverty? To what extent are those truth claims supported by existing research? The study did not examine the instructional strategies that Payne recommends in her book.

Bomer et al. (2007) concluded that

> her work represents a classic example of what has been identified as deficit thinking. We found that her truth claims, offered without any supporting evidence, are contradicted by anthropological, sociological and other research on poverty. We have demonstrated through our analysis that teachers may be misinformed by Payne's claims. As a consequence of low teacher expectations, poor students are more likely to be in lower tracks or lower ability groups and their educational experience is more often dominated by rote drill and practice. (p. 1)

Valencia (1997) writes that deficit thinking is an explanation of school failure among individuals linked to group membership (typically, the combination of racial/ethnic minority status and economic disadvantage). It holds that poor schooling performance is rooted in the children's alleged cognitive and motivational deficits. In this thinking, schools' structure and inequitable schooling arrangements that exclude students from learning are not to blame for the failure. Payne refers to a culture of poverty, with its accompanying attributes of the poor (e.g., family structure, orientation, dysfunctionality, violence, lack of morals, and "hidden rules").

Paul Gorski (2008) in "The Myth of the 'Culture of Poverty,'" suggests that instead of accepting myths that harm low-income students, we need to eradicate the systemwide inequities that stand in their way. He reports that researchers around the world tested the culture of poverty concept empirically. They raised a variety of questions and came to several conclusions about poverty. "But on this they all agree: *There is no such thing as a culture of poverty.* Differences in values and behaviors among poor people are just as great as those between poor and wealthy people" (p. 33).

The appeal of deficit thinking is dependent on a set of values that exist beyond our school doors. It has permeated middle-class U.S. society. When policy constructs poverty as a problem by creating a category for No Child Left Behind (NCLB) called "children of poverty," as a subgroup for assessment accountability, an industry is created to respond to "the problem." As Bomer et al. (2007) state, the industry "consists of many more businesses than just Payne's. Her success indicts us all in education, indeed most of the American public, as it reveals the degree to which we use the education system to protect our own sense of entitlement to privilege." Deficit thinking and the resulting deficit models for improving achievement have been unsuccessful in closing the achievement gaps for children who are economically, culturally, or linguistically diverse. In subsequent chapters, we present an *asset model* of instruction that addresses the achievement gaps and that is responsive to the needs of diverse learners.

Race and Poverty

Looking at the most recent data on students of poverty, we find that although poverty impacts achievement (ES = .76) (Wenglinsky, 2002), there are other factors that have an even greater impact on learning. We know from research (Wenglinsky, 2002) that the effect size of poverty (ES = .76), or the impact on learning of poverty, is 25 percentile points. However, the recent Standardized Testing and Reporting (STAR) results from California (Mangaliman, 2007) indicate that white students who live in poverty are outperforming African American and Latino students who are not poor but who are middle class or affluent. Mangaliman reports that Jack O'Connell, California state superintendent, identified these as "racial gaps," not poverty gaps. This same phenomenon was reported in Pittsburgh (Wereschagin, 2007). Linda Lane, deputy superintendent of the Pittsburgh Public Schools, has responded to a new study led by Robert Strauss of Carnegie Mellon University on the achievement gap. Dr. Lane writes: "Poverty is a factor that affects achievement; however, *race is a larger factor*" (p. 1). This means that something besides poverty is having an even greater impact on learning in our schools.

A recent study by Richard Coley of the Educational Testing Service's (ETS) policy information center (Winerip, 2007), titled "The Family: America's Smallest School," suggests that children of poverty come to kindergarten with a gap. The ETS researchers identified four variables: the percentage of students living with one parent, the percentage of eighth graders absent from school at least three times a month, the percentage of students age five or younger whose parents read to them every day, and the percentage of eighth graders who watch five or more hours of television a day. Using these four variables, they are able to predict state results on the NAEP eighth-grade reading test with impressive accuracy. These four variables account for two-thirds of the large differences among states. Coley suggests that if we're really interested in raising overall levels of achievement and in closing the achievement gap, we need to pay as much attention to the starting line as we do the finish line. For poor children of color, the gaps are even wider. These variables are beyond the control of schools and describe the "deficits" with which children of poverty come to school.

Title I Funding

NCLB has continued to fund a program known as Title I of NCLB to serve students of poverty. Funds are provided to schools based on the number of students who receive free and reduced lunch—an indicator of poverty because it is based on family income. Those students receive additional instruction in reading and mathematics outside the classroom by teachers and assistants paid for by Title I. The program has a parent involvement component that usually involves having parents attend meetings in the evening to learn how to support their children in school. If the percentage of students of poverty is high enough, and the school is not making adequate gains in achievement for their students of poverty, then the school is also required to provide professional development for teachers with a portion of their funds. The emphasis on learning has always been reading and mathematics.

One of the issues for students receiving Title I services has been the lack of coordination between the instructional approach provided by classroom teachers and that provided by Title I teachers. Students who have difficulty mastering reading and mathematics need the most consistency in the approach to instruction, not conflicting ways to learn. Title I should provide additional time to learn, not a time to learn something else. Some districts use their Title I funds to provide literacy coaches and math coaches to support teachers, who in turn are better able to teach their students.

EPE Research Center, *Education Week*'s online newsletter, reports,

> Although Title I is the largest federal elementary and secondary education program, findings about its impact on student achievement have been mixed. Part of the problem has been that Title I is not a specific intervention that can be easily evaluated, but rather a significant funding stream with a large number of requirements that cut across such areas as teacher quality, comprehensive school reform, and curriculum and instruction. Nonetheless, by some accounts, Title I has been credited

with closing the achievement gaps between advantaged and disadvantaged students. From 1970 through the mid-1980s, the learning gap between white students and minority students closed by almost one-third. It is important to note, however, that most of these gains were made in the mastery of basic skills rather than in the mastery of rigorous curricula outlined by state standards. (p. 2)

Another issue is that professional development for teachers does not necessarily focus on research-based, effective instruction that targets the specific standards that are in need of improvement based on low test scores. Training is provided on generic instructional practice. However, the learning needs of the students are specific. For example, in schools we have observed, teachers are provided with training on how to put up a word wall in a primary classroom to help decoding or how to better use the textbook manuals and student workbooks. In these same schools the greatest learning need of students, based on low test scores, is how to summarize and paraphrase what they've read and how to make inferences when reading. The effectiveness (based on research) of the strategies being trained is most often ignored or unknown. Training for Title I teachers is typically a one-size-fits-all workshop. We sometimes refer to them as "shake and bake" solutions. The same information is provided on an instructional practice for everyone, and it is hoped that it has *some* relevancy for all teachers.

Highly Qualified Teachers

High poverty schools that receive funding for Title I are mandated to have "highly qualified teachers" to increase student achievement. The intent of this mandate was good. Peske and Haycock (2006) document that districts and schools often have placed their most inexperienced and weakest teachers in the highest poverty schools.

Children in the highest-poverty schools are assigned to novice teachers almost twice as often as children in low-poverty schools. Similarly, students in high-minority schools are assigned to novice teachers at twice the rate as students in schools without many minority students. Students in high-poverty and high minority schools also are shortchanged when it comes to getting teachers with a strong background in the subjects they are teaching. Classes in high-poverty and high minority secondary schools are more likely to be taught by "out-of-field teachers"—those without a major or minor in the subject they teach. (p. 2)

Teachers begin their work in the district in the poor schools, and when they have enough experience or tenure, they transfer to higher performing schools where teaching is easier.

"Highly qualified teachers" means that these teachers hold a teaching credential and are teaching in the areas in which they are licensed. It is assumed that teachers, by having a credential in the subject area in which they are teaching, have the content knowledge required for that subject. Many state licensing agencies require a subject area test before they will grant a teaching license in a specific subject. There is rarely a requirement that the teachers demonstrate knowledge and skill with effective instruction. There is no requirement that the teacher demonstrate ability to improve achievement. We know that experience with teaching and content knowledge and skill are critical. Even though these are imperfect criteria for defining teachers as highly qualified, there is a body of research that indicates that experience and knowledge of basic subject matter and basic skills do impact student learning. Consequently, when teachers with the least amount of experience and content knowledge are placed with the students in most need of the best teachers, the system "enlarges the achievement gap" (Peske & Haycock, 2006, p. 3). There is no requirement in the definition of "highly qualified" that the teacher demonstrate knowledge and skills with students of poverty or students from diverse cultures.

Afterschool Programs

The bell rings, signaling the end of the school day, and eager students loaded with backpacks head to the row of waiting school buses. However, Marcus (a first grader) and a significant number of his classmates haul their backpacks loaded with homework, notes to parents, permission slips, and schoolwork to another classroom in the school. Marcus and his buddies are heading to programs provided after school.

Marcus is greeted at the door as he enters the double classroom and is asked by his PM teacher how the school day went for him. Students know to respond with a thumbs-up, thumbs-down, or thumbs-sideways signal. Marcus gives her a smile and a thumbs-up. His afterschool program separates students into two groups by grade levels: kindergarten through grade 3 in one room, grades 4–6 in the other room. Marcus knows where to put his backpack so he can go get his afterschool snack and something to drink. "All right! Finally we get chocolate milk!" Marcus picks out a banana, a granola bar, and his favorite—chocolate milk—and joins his study buddies at a table. Music is playing in the background as students talk at their tables with children from several classrooms. This is where they meet to learn and play for up to 20 hours a week.

After everyone has finished their snack, their PM teacher has every child tell something that they have learned more about today. It doesn't have to be about school, and every child has a turn. "I scored in soccer!" "I can now write my last name." "I only missed one spelling word today." "I remembered to feed the kitty this morning." "I learned the *or* sound like in *sword* today." When every child has made his or her contribution, the teacher leads the class in a group cheer for whatever accomplishment that was shared—both personal accomplishments and those as learners. This begins the PM session on a positive tone for the afternoon.

The PM teacher then lays out the agenda for the afternoon. Each task on the agenda is assigned a different color. Groups are established for the afternoon based on tasks to be accomplished by individuals. There is a mix homework, coaching, and practice on needed skills; physical activities; story time; relaxation; art; and music. Children start at different places on the agenda (e.g., homework is blue, story time is yellow, etc.) and rotate through activities in small groups, led by the PM teacher and an assistant. Marcus's group is red today, so he begins his PM class with coaching and practice on skills he has not yet mastered. His classroom teacher provides this information to the PM teacher weekly. Marcus groans. He wanted to work with the Legos first, but he goes with his team to the Coaching and Practice table. He knows that the "third thing" on his agenda will allow him to choose to build with the Legos. He thinks he can wait that long.

This approach has seen some success, depending on how it is structured and staffed. It provides additional instructional time and some guidance and support with homework. Because both parents work in many families, often their children are in afterschool programs. When these programs are staffed with teachers who know for each child what is to be learned, what homework needs to be done, and the individual needs of the students, the time can be used effectively for student learning. When any or all of three elements are missing, the afterschool programs have virtually no effect on the achievement gap.

However, afterschool programs promote a greater commitment to homework, and there is a positive relationship between homework and reading achievement at the national level (U.S. Department of Education, National Center for Education Statistics, 2007).

⧊ Tutoring

When students are in a school that is not making "adequate yearly progress" year after year, they must be provided with an opportunity to learn through additional tutoring. Many private companies have emerged to fill this gap. They have their own curriculum, their own instructional methodology, and their own assessments. Students are confronted with curriculum, instruction, and assessment that may or may not be connected to their learning needs at school. In some districts, classroom teachers are recruited to do additional tutoring after school. However, already burdened teachers find it difficult to add to their full days. Existing data regarding the effectiveness of tutoring for elementary students are limited and inconclusive.

⧊ What's Missing in These Approaches?

None of the approaches (e.g., focusing on curriculum, instruction, and assessment; highly qualified teachers; special funding for students of poverty; tutoring; afterschool programs) have focused on the *learner* and the *learner's culture*. The focus has been on those components of the educational system that historically have been successful in improving achievement for white, middle-class children. And yes, teachers have been incredibly successful with increasing achievement for *white, middle-class children*. Remember the graph showing the California achievement gap by race earlier in the chapter? White children for all grades scored an API index of 801 (an API index of 800 is the goal for proficiency).

The 2006 Program for International Student Assessment (PISA; U.S. Department of Education, 2007) shows U.S. students lagging behind a majority of participating developed nations in both science and mathematics. What is really amazing is another peculiarity of the U.S. education system—a system that, in theory, seeks to provide equal opportunity for all of its children, regardless of economic circumstance. The PISA results (testing 15-year-olds in 57 countries) show that about 18% of the variation in Americans' science scores was related to students' socioeconomic status. This variation was more than twice as high as that of several of the highest-performing countries (e.g., Finland and Canada at 8%). Poverty is less of a factor in higher-scoring nations than in the United States. The PISA results suggest that efforts to maximize performance for all students, even those of poverty, *can* be achieved simultaneously. It should be noted, however, that the top performing countries, while they have fairly diverse economic backgrounds represented by their students, have relatively homogeneous racial and ethnic compositions. In other words, they have similar cultures, and assimilation into the dominant culture by those new to their countries is the norm.

The research shows that American schools tend "to provide students of poverty with less demanding curriculum, poorer-quality teachers, and fewer educational resources than their peers in wealthier U.S. communities," according to Ross Wiener, the vice president of program and policy for the Education Trust, a research and advocacy group in Washington, D.C. (Cavanaugh, 2007, p. 13). This perspective reflects solutions focused on curriculum and instruction to improve achievement.

Culture Trumps Poverty

American schools have not attended to the culture of the learner. Yet it is largely cultural factors that determine what is valued in education, what is motivating to the learner, where the learner will focus his or her attention, what education should accomplish for the learner in his or her context, and the conditions under which the learner best acquires information. Culture trumps poverty in terms of its impact on achievement (Daniels, 2002; Wang & Kovach, 1996; Wang & Reynolds, 1995; Williams 1996, 2003). Achievement data from recent state tests document that culture has a greater impact on the gaps in achievement than does poverty.

Attending to the Collectivist Culture of 70% of the World's Population

What does it mean to address the culture of students? Which cultures do we attend to in our classrooms? When creating a new approach for addressing students of poverty and diverse cultures, how should we change our focus?

Triandis (1990) observed that the emphasis on individualist versus collectivist value systems in schools is probably the most important cultural difference in social behavior that can be identified and suggests that we should be mindful that 70% of the world's population lives in a collective culture. If teachers pay close attention to both the culture of the classroom and incorporating important culture elements of the children, the school becomes more comfortable to both students and teachers. It will also accomplish two goals—focus on increasing achievement and close the achievement gap between white, middle-class students and those living in poverty and from diverse cultures.

Trumbull, Greenfield, and Quiroz (Williams, 2003, pp. 67–93) describe the difference between these two ways of thinking, or value systems—called individualistic and collectivistic—about knowledge, learning, and teaching (Greenfield & Cocking, 1994; Markus & Kitayama, 1991) as they impact learning in classrooms.

First, individualistic classrooms reflect the values of northern European Americans and an Anglo-Saxon heritage. They encourage students to work independently and to do their own work. They reward and recognize individual achievement and show that it is therefore valued. Intelligence is viewed as competitive and aggressive. Students gain knowledge in order to become more competent and able to construct knowledge—which is viewed as power—about the world around them. Valued communication is through linguistic means such as reading and writing. U.S. schools and most European Americans support cognitive development in terms of their knowledge of the physical world and linguistic communication skills. Communication involves talking about the substance, or content, first; relationships to people are second in communications. In other words, when teachers pose a question to their students, the children with northern European ancestry respond with a direct answer to the question related to the content.

Second, collectivist classrooms reflect the value systems of nonmainstream cultures and peoples: Native American Indians, Native Hawaiians, Native Alaskans, Latin Americans, African Americans, Asians, and Arabs. They emphasize the interdependence, as opposed to independence, among the students. There is an emphasis on maintaining relationships that are hierarchically structured around family roles and multiple generations. This means that the family, or community, and a student's place in it supersedes the individual. A child's intelligence is measured by how well he or she knows how to successfully do his or her part in the family and/or community. There is a great deal of value placed on sharing and the ability to participate in social relationships. Knowledge of social responsibility is greatly valued. Communication in collectivist classrooms involves many nonverbal means, such as touching and holding. These classrooms support the child's social intelligence and emphasize interpersonal relationships, respect for elders and tradition, responsibility for others, and cooperation. Communication involves talking about the relationships first, and the content second. In other words, when teachers pose a question to the students, children may respond with the context or relationships affiliated with the content first, and then include the answer to the content the teacher was asking. An example of this might be when Mrs. Telfair, whose class is studying the major food groups, asks her students if they can tell her from which food groups their breakfast that morning came from. Consuelo raises her hand. "My grandma and I always make breakfast. She lets me mix up the eggs and put in some milk and whatever special things I like. Today I picked out some peppers and cheese. We made that with some of Grandma's chorizo. We used the dairy and vegetables and fruit group. We also had some of the meat group and the grain group this morning because we had tortillas, too." Teachers, who often expect the direct answer to their question based on an individualist value system, might get impatient with the long story response. Sometimes they cut the story short because they don't believe the child knows the "correct" response and move on to another student's response. When that happens, do you think the student feels valued? What does that communicate in terms of the teacher's expectations to that child as a learner?

Attending to culture means not making children in our classroom choose between the culture of the home and community and the culture of the classroom. It does not mean that we totally abandon the way we manage our classrooms or deliver instruction. We can honor and provide experiences in our classroom that reflect the cultures of all of our students. We can both provide ample opportunities for students to work together cooperatively (collectivist) and explain that a specific activity is to be done on your own and why (individualistic). We can honor students who answer our curriculum questions by starting to explain the family context in which they learned it before they get to the substance of their answer (collectivist). We can both provide ways for students to share community classroom materials (collectivist) and teach respect for the individual property of a student's desk (individualist). We can both provide times where students respond as a group, such as choral reading, call-and-response techniques, and literature circles (collectivist), and provide opportunities for an individual to respond (individualistic). We can both provide opportunities for movement and touching (collectivist) and provide times where stillness and quiet need to be observed (individualist).

We create culturally responsive classrooms by providing opportunities for different value systems to influence and be incorporated into what is happening in the classroom. This will create classrooms that value, honor, and respect various cultures, and, implicitly, your practices will provide value, honor, and respect to your students.

☖ Contextualizing Curriculum and Instruction

If we want to meet the needs of our students of poverty and diverse cultures, we will want to contextualize, or provide a multicultural context, for the curriculum we are teaching. Haberman (1991) examined classroom instruction for students of poverty. He found that there is an overreliance on a direct instructional model, where teachers teach to the whole class at the same time and control all the classroom discussion and decision making. He calls this approach a "pedagogy of poverty" (Haberman, 1991, p. 290) that leads to complacency, passive resentment, and teacher burnout. What can we do to contextualize our curriculum and instruction?

When choosing instructional practice to improve achievement for students of poverty, we need to attend to five recommendations (Waxman, Padron, & Arnold, 2001)—important because of the differences in background knowledge and experience for children in poverty:

1. We need to guide the thinking process with attention to meaning making. This notion is supported by the work of Brown and DeLoache (1990) in their

work on metacognitive skills. They looked at the application of metacognitive skills for (1) extracting basic information, or the main idea, from texts; (2) visual scanning; and (3) retrieval processes. Teaching children the critical characteristics of different kinds of texts, for example, how informational texts are patterned versus how literary texts are patterned, helps them to strengthen their metacognitive skills for finding the main idea of what they are reading. Explicitly teaching children how to read different kinds of texts, for example, the use of highlighting and underlining for noting significant information, strengthens their metacognitive skills. Both of these—knowledge about the elements of texts and knowledge about how to study different texts—will increase students' ability to make meaning from what they are reading. Visual scanning is another application of metacognitive skills that begins in infancy. It is refined over time to allow students to focus on the more relevant information. Scanning a passage for information requires a strategic action—focusing on the most informative areas, that is, the headers, boldfaced words, to quickly gain information. Using cues to retrieve information, or to remember it, is also an application of metacognitive skills. Initially teachers can provide the cues to remember things and explicitly teach the metacognitive strategy. As students mature, they learn to create their own retrieval cues. Sometimes these are mnemonics like "Every Good Boy Does Fine" (EGBDF) for the names of the lines on a music staff; sometimes they are a hand signal. Vygotsky (1990) reminds us that to support higher level thinking in students, we need to address each child's cultural development if we are to capture the richness of children's thinking and behavior because "the child develops and changes in his/her active adaptation to the external world" (p. 65). He emphasizes that children, in the process of development, use the same forms of behavior in relation to themselves that others initially used in relation to them. That means that where children focus their attention, what they value as a focus for learning, how they learn to express themselves, how they expect to learn, and so on is determined by their socialization in the culture of their family. As teachers guide their students in meaning making, they will want to attend to the cultural values of their children to build better bridges between known (from background knowledge and experience) and new information and learning experiences (presented in school). A child's culture will determine what is relevant in what is learned in school.

2. We need to attend to the context and culture of our students of poverty. This principle is supported by Williams (1996, 2003) and by Zeichner (2003) in *Closing the Achievement Gap*. Zeichner suggests that we "incorporate aspects of our students' languages, cultures, and daily experiences into the academic and social context of schooling" (2003, p. 101) as well as teaching the culture of the classroom so that students can participate fully in the learning process. Both Williams and Zeichner support the concept of cultural responsiveness in instruction, which includes contextualizing and pluralizing the curriculum for culture, providing opportunities for students to work together (i.e., turn taking, peer learning, choral response), and finding ways to bridge the cultures of home and school.

3. We need to use technology at the point of instruction and for demonstrating learning for our digital students. An interesting study was conducted by Derry, Tookey, and Roth (1993), in which they examined the effects on

problem-solving processes with a computer tool called TAPS (which enhances metacognitive activity) with students who worked alone or in groups. The results indicated that students will work four times longer in solving problems collaboratively than alone. Also, when students were allowed to work together, they spent more time in planning and monitoring their learning.

4. We need to provide opportunities for small-group work with individual accountability built into it. The most effective process is that of Johnson, Johnson, and Holubec (1991) in their cooperative learning approach. There are five basic elements of cooperative learning: (a) positive interdependence (students have mutual goals, joint rewards, shared resources, and assigned roles such as summarizer, encourager), (b) face-to-face interaction (students promote each other's learning by helping, sharing, and encouraging face-to-face), (c) individual accountability (where each student's performance is frequently assessed), (d) interpersonal and small-group skills (where students use collaborative skills, such as decision making, communication, and conflict management), and (e) group processing (where groups take time to discuss how well they are achieving their goals and maintaining their relationships). This strategy can be combined with many other learning strategies and can increase achievement by as much as 28 percentile points (Johnson et al., 1991).

5. We need to use strategies that allow students to "think aloud" and to process their thinking together to make meaning. Verbalization is an extremely effective strategy, with an ES of 1.78. In terms of an impact on academic achievement, this means that verbalization will increase achievement by as much as 46 percentile points (Darling, 1999). Verbalization is the practice of encouraging the learners to express the learning and connection-making process to themselves and others through self-talk, voicing thoughts, discussion, thinking, and writing about what is being experienced in the learning process.

The rewards will be increased academic achievement that will close the gap in achievement for our students of poverty—well worth the effort it takes for a paradigm shift.

Critical Elements of an Asset Model

A new model for improving achievement and closing the gaps for students of poverty and diverse cultures will need to address the following elements:

- Collectivist value system
- Motivation and relevance
- Culturally responsive classrooms and context for learning
- Culturally proficient teaching instructional modifications—declarative and procedural knowledge
- Building resilience
- Leadership

Each of these elements will be addressed in subsequent chapters. We will identify specific, research-based instructional strategies that increase learning for children who live in poverty, who are new to this country, and who come from cultures different from our own.

⚛ Ignoring the Problem—Implications

American education is at a crossroads. We can continue to make changes that address the needs of white, middle-class students to improve achievement but that do not address the needs of our increasingly diverse population. However, the consequences for ignoring the educational differences and needs of children of poverty will impact all of us.

For America to maintain its place in a global economy we need all of our children to be productive, contributing members. They not only need to graduate from high school but also need training and education beyond in order to compete. We must create the conditions in our K–12 schools to allow entry into postsecondary institutions—a means of entry to the middle class for our students of poverty. We need an educated citizenry, with a substantial middle class, to sustain a democracy. We must meet the different needs of our students of poverty in order for them to acquire the knowledge and skills required in a digital society. We can no longer accept the old paradigm model that holds low expectations for students of poverty. We can no longer blame the students, the system, or the educators. We know what works; we need the moral courage to implement it.

Students of poverty who are not provided an education that builds resilience to overcome the circumstances of their birth are not given the opportunity to contribute the assets that they bring—economically, politically, and socially—to this country. We need to invest in them, learn from them, and we will all benefit. Students of poverty who do not achieve in school drain our social services and our health care system and fill our prisons. In the country with the most abundance and wealth, we can no longer educationally address only the needs of middle-class, European-American students. Our educational system needs to provide equal access to a quality education for all of its children. We all deserve no less.

Subsequent chapters will provide you with the knowledge and tools to answer this teacher's plea described in the following scenario.

> "I got a new student after the holidays. He's adorable, and I think he's pretty bright because of the speed with which he assesses a situation. I also think he's very street-wise. He is African American and Puerto Rican, and while he speaks English, it's not the English we read, write, and speak in our school. His speech is laced with swearing and foul language. I've tried to indicate that we don't talk like that in class, but he ignores me. I'm worried that other students will pick it up, or worse, tell their parents. He seems to be observing and sizing me and his classmates up since he got here last week. He comes into the classroom loudly every morning. He
>
> *(Continued)*

(Continued)

makes the rounds of the groups of students in the room, telling stories, touching them, and making sure they notice that he is here. The other students seem to see him as a leader and sometimes copy his behavior. When it's time for the day to begin, he ignores my directions about sitting at his desk and listening. I have to actually begin to move in his direction for him to sit down. Then, he gives me one of those radiating smiles that melt your heart. During reading, he either puts his head down on the desk, refusing to even open the book, or he begins to wander around the room, touching everything. When he does attempt to do a worksheet or to read for me, I can tell he is way behind the other students. Everything I've tried to engage him in reading and math has not worked. Nobody seems to know where this student went to school before here. He dresses sloppy and keeps 'forgetting' to bring a coat.

"Our school is a High Priority School because we've not made enough gains in achievement in this high poverty school. We have to get our students to Basic Proficiency on the reading tests or they will close our school. I've been teaching for 12 years, and I believe I'm a good teacher. It's January, and I don't know what to do with this boy."

Motivation From Within 2

Ask any teacher what they wish they could change about their students, and the word *motivation* is sure to come up. How does one motivate students to learn? We have bad news and good news. The bad news is that no one can motivate *you* but you. No one can motivate your students but your students themselves; motivation comes from within. The good news is that, thanks to brain research, we now know ways to activate our students' natural motivation in the brain. To understand how motivation works, let's look at some current brain research.

We like Marzano's model because it is a concise way to explain a complicated process. He calls the thinking system of the brain involved in motivation the "self-system" of the brain. It is not one location in the brain but a combination of areas that impact motivation. In college, most of us were taught to begin our lessons with the information—usually the facts—first (declarative knowledge), and then the skills and processes second (procedural knowledge). However, the brain does not begin learning in the cognitive system, which addresses the domains of declarative and procedural knowledge, but always begins in the self system. This is the part of the brain that says, "Do I wanna?" Students who have not had positive experiences with learning before, or who do not have a positive relationship with the teacher, very likely will not want to pay attention. Students who come from the Anglo-Saxon European background or who feel comfortable in schools that run on that model may be able to grab the learning from the beginning. However, students from a collectivist culture— which includes most of the world—will have difficulty identifying the internal desire to learn until the needs of the self-system are met. As a teacher in a typical middle-class-directed classroom, you may be starting your lessons in the cognitive system, focusing on goals and objectives from your content, but we assure you that only your highly motivated students are with you. When you present a learning task, most learners are focused on questions such as "Do I want to pay attention?" "What is in it for me personally?" "What does this have to do with me?" "Do I care?" "Can I be successful?" "How do I feel about this class, this teacher, and this subject?" In about 15 seconds, they make the decision to pay attention or not. These are the questions the brain asks before it chooses to engage in any learning task.

In the paragraphs that follow we explain the significance of each of the questions that play an important part in their motivation to pay attention, to learn, and to engage in the learning.

≫ How Do I Feel About the Classroom, the Teacher, or the Subject Matter?

In Chapter 1 we discussed some basic differences between the typical Caucasian, middle-class student of European descent and students from other cultures. In that chapter we maintained that for students of European descent, the substance (in this case, the learning content) comes first, and relationships with the teacher and their fellow students come after. For all other cultures, the relationship must be established first. Teachers from the European, middle-class culture have trouble understanding why it is so important to build the relationship first. They may even consider it a waste of time in an atmosphere where "covering the subject is paramount."

We still have nightmares over a first grader who missed the school bus that stopped in front of the administration building where we worked. He came in crying because he had missed the bus. Of course, we arranged to take him to his elementary school, but in the meantime, we talked to him. He was shaking with fear over being late to school, and he said through his sobs that his teacher didn't like him. An investigation proved that he was correct. His teacher taught primarily middle-class Caucasian children, and he was a child of color. She did not understand or know how to deal with him. After a meeting with her, she decided to take early retirement. While we saved one school life, we despair over the many others like him who go to school in a hostile environment for whatever reason. While we thankfully admit that this teacher with her built-in prejudice toward anyone who did not look like her is not typical of teachers in this country, we also know that caring teachers who are not of color and who are of the dominant culture in a school are often frustrated because their diverse learners are not responding to the classroom, to them, or to the material presented. For most cultures, relationship must be established first.

Students who have failed math over and over will probably approach math with fear and dread. Students who have had a negative experience with a teacher will not enter the classroom full of joy to be there. A classroom can be a hostile environment just as a workplace may be in the "real world."

For students from poverty, self-efficacy is the gatekeeper to motivation. Self-efficacy is wrapped up in how the student feels about the learning, and it is based on past experience. In the last century, a great deal of emphasis was placed on self-esteem. We believed it was important that students feel good about themselves—and it is important for all students. Self-esteem is built on "I am loveable and I am capable." Self-esteem says, "I feel good about myself and I believe that I can do this work." While that is important, self-efficacy is more powerful because it is built on past experience. Self-efficacy says, "This math is hard, but I know I can do it because I have been successful before." That old adage, "Success breeds success," is absolutely true. Self-efficacy is more powerful because it is built on fact. As a matter of fact, self-efficacy is often called the "gatekeeper" to motivation.

While self-efficacy is built by success in the classroom, it is built only by authentic success. What do we mean by this? In the last century, many educators, in an effort to promote self-esteem, were directed to "water down" the curriculum so that more students could experience success. However, providing a curriculum without rigor does not lead to greater self-esteem or to self-efficacy. Students usually know when they are being given less challenging work, and it does not make them feel better about themselves. As educators, we must remember that all students deserve a "quality" education that is rigorous and prepares them for the future.

What Is the Personal Importance of the Learning?

For something to be important to us, it will usually be perceived either as instrumental in satisfying a basic need or as instrumental in the attainment of a personal goal. Will learning this help me to look better to my friends? Will learning this help me to get into a class or program that is important to me? Will learning this keep me from being cheated on the streets? To tap into importance, know your students and what they deem to be important in their lives. What is important to your diverse learners is determined by their culture. Understanding their cultural context will help you to identify what is significant to your students.

Another aspect of personal importance is real-world application. Students may perceive that the learning has no application outside the classroom and decide to tune it out. Have you ever had students in your classroom ask you, "When are we ever going to use this in the real world?" They are on overload; if they are not going to use it outside the classroom, they may memorize for the test on Friday and then promptly forget it—or they may choose not to learn it at all. My favorite math teacher, who teaches higher level math, has a sign in her classroom that reads, "I will never teach you something in this classroom for which I cannot give you the real-world application." She not only shows students how they will use the math in the real world but also makes that authentic application a part of the learning, and they demonstrate that use whenever possible. For example, students learning angles in math created the angles for angled parking near the school under the supervision of the Department of Transportation. Students studying slope examined and reported the angles used for handicap ramps in and around the school using the federal guidelines for the angles of ramps. (Not all of the ramps met federal guidelines.) If you have seen the wonderful math series, *Good Morning, Mrs. Toliver* (PBS, 1993), you may remember that Mrs. Toliver introduced fractions to her students by bringing pizza dough to school and by discussing how pizza is cut into fractional parts. She reminded her students that they could get cheated easily when buying pizza if they did not understand the difference in a pizza cut in eights as compared with a pizza cut in fourths.

Science students in one of our high schools studied the impact of amusement park rides on the human body. In studying the history of the roller coaster, they found that in the early years people often got whiplash, or worse, from riding roller coasters that were created by people not aware of g-forces and their effects on the body. Students worked in small groups to create amusement park rides, taking into account the physics skills they had learned. Using software for that purpose, students applied the software to their projects to determine the effects at various points of the ride on the body. Part of their grade on the project was to create a ride that would not be harmful. We believe that these students will be much more likely to remember the physics lessons they learned in this project than they would if they had simply read the information in the text or received it by lecture from the teacher.

In his book, *Teaching Reading to Black Adolescent Males: Closing the Achievement Gap* (2005), Alfred Tatum explains that black males may regard reading as a passive female activity or may find that the literature offered in schools leans more toward female or less masculine heroes at a time when he is moving from childhood to manhood and seeking masculine identity. Tatum reminds teachers to focus on gender awareness and an emphasis on masculinity when making choices for reading in a classroom with adolescent black males. He offers the following suggestions:

- Use male-oriented texts with male characters (as opposed to more female-oriented texts).
- Use texts that are apt to engage boys emotionally with the characters that deal with issues boys care about, and that honor their identity.
- Expose boys to nonfiction that involves learning something new.
- Use texts that legitimize the male experience and support boys' view of themselves. (p. 11)

We realize that certain literature pieces are required from early childhood through grade 12 and that the real world of teaching means that we must find ways to make those literature choices appealing to students who may not see the relevance in the learning.

One key to making the reading personally relevant is to help students learn empathy or to see the connection between characters in literature and people they encounter in their lives. In Daniel Pink's book, *A Whole New Mind* (2005), we are told that in this century our students will be marketable if they can do what computers cannot. He lists the following skills as part of the new literacy:

1. *The ability to show empathy.* This does not mean that we agree with the person but that we have the ability to listen to his or her side of the story and to see how he or she could come to the decisions that he or she does—whether we agree with those choices or actions or not.

2. *The ability to explain in a contextual format.* Most of the world learns through context or stories. For many of your students who are not from a European, Anglo-Saxon background, this is the way they learn best. In middle-class America we often learn through a linear, step-by-step fashion. As we move to a global world, it is important that we acknowledge and build on our students' ability to explain in a story format. For example, a teacher in a typical

middle-class setting might ask students for the parts of an apple, expecting her students to provide a linear list such as peel, core, seeds, and so on. This same teacher might be surprised when she calls on a Hispanic student who answers in a story format about how she helps her mother in the kitchen to peel apples. If the teacher is not aware of the cultural differences in answering the question, she might mistakenly think that the Hispanic child does not know the answer or does not understand the question. Most of the students from cultures outside of the European, Anglo-Saxon background bring this gift to the table. Help them to hone it and use it to help others understand concepts.

3. *The ability to see the big picture.* Students will need to be able to see the inter-connectedness of things. In the wonderful book *If a Butterfly Sneezes,* we are reminded that a disaster or change in weather patterns or extinction of an animal in India or China or California affects us all. Students from poverty often focus on the here and now and must be directly taught to see the connections. This is also a way to help the classroom teacher make the learning relevant. For example, can we look at a character such as Hamlet and draw conclusions about human nature and choices that people make? Have we known people who have some of the same characteristics or who have made some of the same kinds of choices?

4. *The ability to use humor.* In some cultures humor is considered a gift. The people who can make us laugh are often the most popular. Build on this in the classroom by adding humor to the lessons. Use cartoons, video clips, music, pictures, and so on to bring the student's attention back to the learning. When we train teachers and administrators, we often use short video clips that lead into our topic. For example, we use a wonderful video clip of Ma and Pa Kettle explaining why 25 divided by 5 is 5. Ma and Pa Kettle believe it is 14 and set out to prove it. We use this as a lead-in to discussing modalities of learning such as visual, kinesthetic, and auditory. Students who "don't get it" over and over may not ever get it until they are taught in the modality most comfortable to them. In the Ma and Pa Kettle clip, their son is trying to show them why 25 divided by 5 is 5 rather than 14, and when they don't get it he reteaches in the same modality. He reteaches several times, each time in the same modality—visual. They never "get it." The son finally gives up. This example both uses humor and teaches a concept in a context.

5. *A sense of meaning.* Those who can see beyond everyday circumstances to find meaning and purpose in life will have the ears of the twenty-first century. Resilience has a direct correlation to a sense of meaning. We will talk about resiliency throughout this book.

Social knowledge and skills are valued by collectivist cultures and are perceived as assets. As a teacher, tap into these assets to meet these expectations.

Tatum (2005) also talks about the work of researchers Michael Smith and Jeffrey Wilhelm (2002) who found that even when black adolescent boys saw the importance of the learning, they often rejected it because it did not relate to their immediate interests and needs. They preferred text that opened up conversations, that was about real events, and that showed more than one perspective. This perception of the learning condition might be called "flow." Tatum (paraphrasing

Csikszentmihalyi, 1990) lists the following four conditions as making up the flow experience:

1. There is a feeling of control.

2. The activities provide an appropriate level of challenge.

3. Clear goals and feedback are included.

4. The focus is on the immediate. (2006, p. 13)

⁂ Emotion and Learning

It is thought that emotion is one of the strongest forces in the brain; it can literally shut down our learning process, or it can enhance it. The emotional response that a student brings to the new task will help shape the degree of motivation associated with that task.

We want to make the classroom and school environment such that students never feel threatened either emotionally or physically. Emotional threats take place when we

• do not give students the scaffolding they need to be successful. This might include clear directions, adequate time to practice the learning, and clear and written expectations for the learning that includes rubrics provided up front before the assignment. We need to explicitly teach the organizational skills they need to be successful, slowly withdrawing the support as they become more capable. Scaffolding support is critical in all tasks in learning. Teachers provide the patterns for learning new tasks. The brain likes novelty, but it also needs patterns that are consistent, such as in the way we grade or carry out expectations. What is true today should be true tomorrow, and it should be true for all students. We recommend that teachers use rubrics for everything that they ask students to do for a grade. After all, how will students know if they are meeting the expectations for quality work if they are not provided with a clear idea of what is expected—and in writing—from mid-elementary school through grade 12. Figure 2.1 is an example of a rubric for a homework assignment for a written essay. We also suggest consistency among teachers. If a rubric for math homework is provided by one teacher, shouldn't it hold true for math homework throughout the school's classrooms?

• treat students unfairly or allow other students to treat a student unfairly. This also includes having low expectations for students of poverty. Benard (1996) states, "Research clearly shows that teacher education students who are mostly white and monolingual tend to view diversity of student backgrounds as a problem rather than as a resource that enriches teaching and learning" (p. 58). A climate of fairness and respectful behavior is critical for students to develop trust. Our goal should be to build resiliency in our students from poverty.

Parts (Essentials)	Points	Attributes (Qualities)
Thesis statement		☐ Clear position taken ☐ Logical
Introduction		☐ Attention grabbing ☐ Thesis statement—last sentence
Voice		☐ Targets intended audience
Reasons		☐ Three reasons clearly stated in topic sentence(s) ☐ Emotion/logic based
Support/Elaboration		☐ Transition statements as links ☐ Supported with examples/other elaboration techniques ☐ Clinchers
Conclusions		☐ Restates position statement ☐ Reestablishes reasons ☐ Includes call to action

Figure 2.1 Homework Matrix for a Persuasive Essay

Resiliency— Why It Matters 3

Most educators with children of poverty in their classrooms, particularly if they are teaching in an area of concentrated poverty, know some of the conditions under which their students live. Their students bring different experiences to their classrooms. Many of their students know somebody who has been killed in their neighborhoods; they know what it's like not to have mittens or boots in cold climates; they know how to prepare to leave their living quarters in 20 minutes with all of their belongings; some know how to forage and stash food; they know how to disguise what has been received from charity; and some know that you need to worry that the heat might be turned off in the winter. They are very aware of the people and relationships that surround them in the here and now. McKinney, Flenner, Frazier, and Abrams (2006), in their research on students in concentrated poverty, note, "The effects of family poverty are exacerbated when there is a high concentration of low-income families and individuals in the neighborhood. Known as 'collective socialization,' depressed attitudes and motivation may be accepted as normative, thereby reducing urban children's expectations and hope for the future, and success in school" (p. 2). Neither the students nor their teachers have the power to change the conditions under which students live. The challenge before teachers, and what they *do* have power to control, is to create the educational conditions for these students to succeed in spite of the adverse circumstances under which they live. When teachers create these conditions, they build resilience in their students to succeed in school, create hope and belief in their students as persons and as learners, help students aspire to some form of postsecondary education, and provide their students with the key to override the impact of poverty. Most schools believe that they need to focus solely on strengthening curriculum, instruction, and assessment to improve achievement for students. However, in order to engage our students of poverty in learning tasks, it is critical that we focus on the learner, to build the resilience in the learner, so he or she can maximize the learning opportunities presented by the teacher with the strengthened curriculum, instruction, and assessment to improve achievement. If we cannot eliminate the conditions of poverty, how can we protect children from its effects so that they can succeed? How can we build resilience in the child?

Poverty influences children's perceptions, interactions, and relationships. Haberman (1995, 2005) identifies five areas that impact urban children affected by concentrated poverty. Children living in concentrated poverty may (a) have difficulty trusting adults, (b) avoid interacting with others, (c) demonstrate feelings of hopelessness, (d) reveal as little as possible about themselves, and (e) respond only by giving and taking orders. These perceptions, interactions, and relationships impact how children approach learning.

What Is Resiliency?

Waxman, Gray, and Padron (2003), in their review of research on educational resilience, define resilient students as those who succeed in school despite the presence of adverse conditions. Benard (1996) refers to resilient students as children who successfully adapt despite risk and adversity. Four traits that she identified in her work with resilient students are social competence, problem-solving skills, autonomy, and a sense of purpose and future.

A review of these traits identified by Benard allows us to examine strategies that teachers can develop to respond to students in poverty that will build resilience in them to succeed in spite of adverse conditions.

Social Competence

Social competence requires that students know the appropriate behavior for the place where and for the people with whom they are interacting. We call these relationship skills. Resilient students are responsive and have the ability to elicit positive responses from other people. They are flexible and have the ability to move back and forth between their primary culture and that of the dominant culture. They are also able to show empathy, are caring, have good communication skills, and have a sense of humor.

Problem-Solving Skills

Resilient students have the ability to plan. They are good at asking for help from others. They can think critically, creatively, and reflectively. They try out different solutions to both cognitive and social problems. Resilient students are aware of the obstacles they face—whether an insensitive school or teacher, an alcoholic parent, or a racist society—and they have developed strategies for overcoming them.

Autonomy

Autonomy is a sense of one's own identity and involves an ability to act independently. Resilient students believe they have some control over their environment. They have a sense that they can master a task. Resilient students have a belief in themselves as both a person and a learner, that is, self-efficacy. They do not believe the negative messages sent to them about themselves or their culture. They can distance themselves from what they believe to be dysfunctional, that is, parental, school, or community dysfunction. This protects them.

Sense of Purpose and Future

Resilient students have goals and educational aspirations, and they are motivated to achieve. They are persistent in getting their needs met. They are optimistic and hopeful. Benard (1996) reports on lifespan studies conducted by Werner and Smith (1992) which document that human beings have an innate capacity to adapt to their circumstances. They "offer us a more optimistic outlook than the perspective that can be gleaned from the literature on the negative consequences of perinatal trauma, care-giving deficits, and chronic poverty" (Benard, 1996, p. 202).

The literature on urban school effectiveness (Edmonds, 1986; Rutter, Maughan, Mortimore, Ouston, and Smith, 1979) corroborates the research on resiliency. The literature identifies clear categories of interventions that teachers can use that will foster resiliency in students to overcome the odds. Benard (1996) calls these "protective factors" (p. 100). These protective factors seem to change the potential negative outcomes for children and help them to overcome the adverse conditions in which they live.

John Vitto, in *Relationship-Driven Classroom Management: Strategies That Promote Student Motivation* (2003), examines the protective factors that similarly impact resilience. He identifies the same external protective factors that are present outside the student and involve the family and school environment as those identified by Benard (1996): care and support, setting high expectations, and encouraging meaningful roles or opportunities for active participation. However, Vitto also identifies internal protective factors, or social-emotional skills, that are characteristics or attributes that the student possesses. These internal factors are

1. Social skills such as self-awareness, empathy, communication skills, and conflict-management skills

2. Problem-solving skills such as the ability to generate alternative solutions and the ability to engage in abstract and flexible thought

3. Self-control such as the ability to delay gratification and regulate mood and the ability to think about consequences before acting

4. Self-efficacy, which is the belief that they can have an influence on their own life and that they can accomplish their own goals

5. Optimism, such as having hope for a better future, being goal directed and persistent, and being able to provide a nonnegative explanation of events

Vitto believes that teachers can foster resilience by having a positive relationship with their students. Teachers can impact students' resilience by building social-emotional competencies such as self-awareness, self-regulation, motivation, empathy, and social skills. To overcome adversity (e.g., friendship problems, divorce, illness, death of friends or loved ones, loss of job, moving, accidents, abuse, alcoholism, robberies, etc.) our students need teachers who communicate that they care by listening, by being compassionate, and by establishing personal and positive relationships that go beyond the classroom. This helps students believe that they are cared for and worthwhile. Strategies that teachers can use are relationship building, classroom community building, social skills training, mentoring, advisory groups, and creating a school within a school in large systems.

Teachers who recognize their students' strengths and interests use these as starting points for building resilience. They examine the strengths more extensively than they search for deficits. Teachers can then build time into their students' schedules to work in their areas of strength and interest. Teachers need to provide challenge and hold high expectations for their students by offering a varied curriculum and diverse instructional formats (e.g., teacher directed, cooperative learning, small groups, etc.). We can value different ways of learning and allow student participation, choice, and decision making in areas that impact the classroom. Teachers can help their students to be more optimistic by helping them to not take adversity personally so that they don't blame themselves. Teachers can help students see problems and adversity as a temporary situation.

Both Vitto and Benard recommend that teachers provide many opportunities for students to engage in meaningful roles and responsibilities in the classroom, to express their opinions, to give back to their community—both in and out of school—and to have a voice in curriculum planning and rule development for the classroom. Examples of these opportunities are engaging students in environmental issues such as setting up a recycling program, contributing to a charitable organization with time and fund-raising, reading to younger children, taking care of classroom plants or animals, and any other number of activities to enhance the belief that "I am important and I can contribute in meaningful ways."

We know what resiliency is, and we know the characteristics of resilient students. We now turn to what teachers can do to foster resilience in students.

☙ Implications for Practice

In *The Freedom Writers Diary* (1999), a book consisting of diary entries from 150 high school students in a high poverty school, one of the students writes about a confrontation with her teacher. The student had self-evaluated herself with a grade of "F." She had missed a lot of school because her mom had a debilitating disease, and she had to help take care of her brothers and sisters. Her teacher, Erin Gruwell, would not accept that self-evaluation and let the student know that, under no circumstances, was she going to allow the student to fail.

In the student's words,

> She was not going to let me fail, even if that meant coming to my house every day until I finished the work. I couldn't tell her off, so I just stood there with tears in my eyes. What she showed me today is that a truly self-reliant person takes action, leaving nothing to chance and everything to themselves. She showed me that excuses will not bring about success and

that adversity is not something you walk with, but something you leap over. The only obstacles are the ones you allow. A chain is only as strong as its weakest link. A truly self-reliant person finds his weak link and strengthens it. I want to be a self-reliant person, now and forever. (p. 120)

Caring and Support

The first "protective factor" that Benard (1996) identifies is caring and support. The aforementioned diary entry of the student who gave herself an "F" exemplifies how resilience can result from a caring and supportive teacher. Often, schools are a refuge for many children, and they provide a protective shield for students in their quest to succeed in spite of the hardships that they face. "Caring in schools is seeing possibilities in each child and using one's wisdom of the heart" (Benard, 1996, p. 103). It means holding high expectations for every student and being able to reflect back the gifts that you see in the student. It lets them hear that you believe in them and that you care enough to not give up on them.

Werner and Smith (1992) write, "The resilient youngsters in our study all had at least one person in their lives who accepted them unconditionally, regardless of temperamental idiosyncrasies, physical attractiveness, or intelligence" (p. 205). To show caring and support, teachers can carefully listen to their students' stories. Listening attentively is a powerful signal that a teacher cares about them. Teachers can also demonstrate caring by demonstrating kindness, compassion, and respect. They should demonstrate that they don't judge their students, and they don't take students' behavior personally. They should convey that they understand that their students are doing the best they can to get through hardships.

Henderson and Milstein (1996) identify ways in which teachers can foster resiliency. Teachers can create opportunities for students to bond with one another. Cooperative learning, active learning, peer tutoring, and student mentoring programs all provide opportunities for students to build interdependent, caring relationships.

Schools build resiliency by creating an environment of caring and personal relationships. If we are to create a climate of caring for students, it means that teachers, too, must have caring support networks. Collegial support is key to sustaining change in a school, but it is also a key variable leading to higher student achievement (McLaughlin & Talbert, 1993). This is especially true in schools serving students from diverse cultures and for students living in poverty.

Positive and High Expectations

Henderson and Milstein (1996) also include high and reasonable expectations as one of the ways in which teachers build resiliency in students. "Urban children are likely to be victims of labels, which communicate and foster low expectations. When a teacher demonstrates an attitude of low expectations, this can produce a negative *Pygmalion Effect* (Rosenthal & Jacobson, 1968) or self-fulfilling prophecy" (McKinney et al., 2006, p. 6). Teachers' high expectations can structure and guide student behavior. Teachers with high expectations get students to reach beyond what they think they can do. They do this by focusing on the strengths of students. They assist those who have been labeled by schools or oppressed by their families or communities. These teachers help students use their "personal power to transform themselves from victims to survivors" (Waxman et al., 2003, p. 12). Teachers who can do this are student centered. They help their students to see that the adversity in their lives is not permanent, but rather is an obstacle that is temporary and that they can overcome.

In the example of the student who was missing school to help her disabled mother care for her younger brothers and sisters, the high expectations of her teacher were clearly communicated, coupled with enough caring and support for the student to believe that she could succeed in spite of the circumstances.

Benard (1996) reminds us that teachers with high expectations help to keep students from using alcohol and drugs, decrease the number of students who drop out of school, and increase the number of students who go on to college. Teachers communicate these high expectations by letting students know that the work they assign is important, that they believe students can do it, and that they won't give up on them. This means creating personal relationships between teachers and students.

Teachers who have high expectations believe that their students have potential. They can convey this belief by taking time to let each child know that they believe in him or her—both as a person and as a student. They develop their self-esteem and self-efficacy in meaningful ways. Teachers who teach to a broad range of learning styles and multiple intelligences communicate that they value the gifts that each student brings. However, as Hilliard (1989) concludes after years of studying the role of learning and teaching style in the education of youths of color,

> The explanation for the low performance of culturally different minority group students will not be found by pursuing questions of behavioral style. . . . The children, no matter what their style, are failing primarily because of systematic inequities in the delivery of whatever pedagogical approach the teachers claim to master—not because students cannot learn from teachers whose styles do not match their own. (p. 68)

Holding high expectations overrides teaching and learning style and makes a significant difference in learning.

We can communicate our high expectations for students in the ways in which we group them in our classrooms. Putting children in heterogeneous, cooperative learning groups where each child holds a significant role in the learning communicates that we expect them to be able to contribute significantly to the tasks assigned to the group. Benard (1996) also suggests that infusing multicultural content throughout the curriculum leads to high expectations and resiliency. "This honors students' home cultures, gives them the opportunity to study their own and other cultures, and helps them develop cultural sensitivity" (p. 109).

How teachers handle evaluation in their classrooms can also demonstrate high or low expectations. Assessment can be a solitary experience where judgments are sometimes manifested about a student.

A positive example of how to effect constructive evaluation can be seen in Mrs. Cabral's first/second-grade classroom in Sacramento. Her classroom is full of six- and seven-year-old children eager to see their assessment results. They ask when the next test will be given so they can show what they've learned. "Can we do it again tomorrow?" Mrs. Cabral's classroom is in an area of extreme poverty, with a very high percentage of her students new to this country and from different cultures. Why are they so eager to be assessed?

Like all of the other teachers in her school, Mrs. Cabral administers formative assessments assigned by the district. What is different is that she approaches assessment with these children not as a tool to label or sort her students but as a tool from which she and they can learn. Mrs. Cabral always lets her children know what they are going to be learning and how she and they will know it before every lesson. There is an expectation in the classroom that all students will learn the knowledge or skill. The classroom culture allows for students to help each other in the learning process. It also provides an opportunity to prepare for the assessments together before the assessment is individually administered. Mrs. Cabral meets with the children in small groups to analyze the language of questions together. They analyze together the format of the answers. The content to be measured is also analyzed together, with students cheering each other as correct responses are given. Misconceptions are identified as an "a-ha" moment. She praises the students for sharing them, and the group does a quick compare and contrast between the misconception and the more accurate response to identify where the misunderstandings occurred. The children perceive themselves as learners in the process. They tell her, "Let me try again! I've got it now!"

Mrs. Cabral's students have learned from her that she expects every single one of them to achieve proficiency on the test. She will work with them one-on-one, they can help each other, and they can work in groups. The high expectation is still that everyone in this class can be proficient. The results of her assessments are shared with the class as a whole group. With simple graphical representations, students can see their results as a class—this is a class goal, not an individual goal. There are bars on the graph for every learner outcome, although student names are not listed on the graph. The marks on the left side indicate the levels of proficiency. The class can see what they know and what they still need to learn. The areas where the class is scoring low are examined as a group. They look at the question to see what it is asking, how it was like or unlike their practices, and then Mrs. Cabral goes over the answer and the errors. She does not identify who made the error at that time. The class analyzes the errors to see if there is an "a-ha" moment for them. No student is singled out, labeled, or shamed. You can watch the understanding blossom in their faces. They are learning—using assessment as the vehicle. It is true that some students are going to need one-on-one attention, and it *is* hard for her to find time. Sometimes she has to tell her students that she didn't teach a particular item very well and that she'll teach it again so that they have another opportunity to learn. (Note, it isn't that *they* didn't learn well enough; it is that *she* didn't teach well enough.) However, these students are consistently meeting their expectations in both math and reading assessments and are often exceeding them. Mrs. Cabral's students achieve proficiency over and over again, both individually and collaboratively as a class. It is heartening to see the cheers of success on each next try. High expectations are driving learning through assessment.

※ Providing Opportunities for Meaningful Participation

Henderson and Milstein (1996) suggest that teachers can foster resiliency when they provide meaningful opportunities for students to contribute their skills and energies. As teachers, we provide opportunities to participate and contribute by allowing students to express their opinions, make choices, problem solve, work with and help others, and give back to their community.

Benard (1996) states, "Participating in decisions about one's life and future is a fundamental human need, closely tied to the need to have some power over one's life" (p. 111). If we don't provide choices for students in school, we are ignoring this need and making the school environment alienating. Our challenge is to engage all children's innate desire and ability to learn and participate in meaningful activities and roles. This is especially important for students who live in poverty, or for those whose families may have been excluded from fully participating in the social, economic, and political life of this country.

A review of the literature on effective instructional practices (Benard, 1996, 2003; Cole, 1995; McKinney et al., 2006; Waxman et al., 2001; Waxman et al., 2003) reveals a consensus on these strategies as particularly effective for diverse learners because they address their cultural needs, values, and beliefs:

- Involving students in curriculum planning
- Self-evaluation strategies
- Critical thinking skills
- Teaching for relevancy
- Cooperative learning
- Culturally responsive teaching
- Incorporating technology
- Instructional conversations
- Differentiating instruction

Given that these strategies that will address specific cultural needs and provide meaningful experiences to build resilience for children living in poverty and from diverse cultures, let's explore the effective research-based instructional strategies that teachers can use in the classroom that will address these recommendations. The instructional strategies are drawn from the Learning Bridges Aligned Instructional Database, with their impact on student learning drawn from that research (Darling, 1999; used with permission of Learning Bridges). The following effective strategies have an impact on learning for all children; however, not all strategies with a high impact on achievement work well with diverse learners. The highly effective strategies that we have chosen to share in this book are those that specifically address the cultural needs of diverse learners, including those living in poverty.

Critical Thinking Skills

Critical thinking competencies are strategies to increase student effectiveness in learning through analyzing, synthesizing, evaluating, and drawing inferences. Critical thinking will enable learners to

- Make insightful interpretations of new information and develop justification for conclusions
- Develop strategies of predicting, gathering information, classifying, organizing, supporting inferences, and justifying conclusions appropriate to the context and audience
- Learn specific thinking processes
- Internalize and analyze learned information

When using critical thinking skills, the teacher will

- Challenge learners with closed or open-ended problems and situations
- Model and verbalize high-level thinking and problem-solving processes
- Encourage thinking and evaluation while reading, writing reports and expositions, and note taking such as mapping and diagramming
- Provide real-life information and events that are relevant to the learner
- Honor, encourage, and accept collaboration, divergent points of view, creative insights, and fresh solutions
- Embed processes for critical thinking and evaluation into content on a continuous basis

Critical thinking skills will increase learning by as many as 41 percentile points (Darling, 1999).

Teaching for Relevancy

Teaching for relevancy provides a real-life, authentic application for the student's learning during the teaching and learning process. Teaching for relevancy will enable learners to

- Actively engage in the learning by connecting to real-life situations
- Process the new learning into long-term memory because it will be more meaningful to them
- Activate prior knowledge about the topic being learned
- Use products and other real-life, authentic means to demonstrate an understanding
- Generalize the learning to new situations
- Use advanced organizers to illustrate connections between new and known knowledge
- Reflect on the new learning through speaking and writing

When using teaching for relevancy, the teacher will

- Provide applications from the real world—outside of school—as an application for students to demonstrate their learning
- Integrate the curriculum to reflect the authentic application of the learning

- Prompt students to activate prior knowledge about the topic
- Provide products, projects, and other real-life, authentic means for students to demonstrate their knowledge of the topic
- Encourage the use of advanced organizers to assist students in making the connections between new and known knowledge
- Provide specific feedback on student demonstrations of learning
- Provide an opportunity for self-reflection on the learning to embed the new knowledge

Teaching for relevancy will increase learning by as many as 40 percentile points (Darling, 1999).

Cooperative Learning

Cooperative learning is a strategy that involves student participation in small groups to maximize learning for themselves and others. Cooperative learning will enable learners to

- Work in groups to achieve a task
- Communicate with each other and help one another with learning tasks, problems, and ideas
- Show individual and group accountability by taking responsibility for their personal contribution, individual learning, and whole-group performance
- Develop appropriate social skills for working with others
- Process their achievement within the group and monitor and evaluate the results

When using cooperative learning, the teacher will

- Explain, model, and guide how to think critically and how to work collaboratively
- Compose groups, furnish resources, and structure tasks so that students must depend on one another for their personal, teammates', and groups' success
- Ensure that the process and product is intrinsically interesting to the students
- Provide a resource-rich, positive, and safe environment for students to achieve individual and group goals
- Facilitate and encourage the positive and productive interaction of all team members
- Help students adapt and/or clarify their shared and individual goals
- Provide the time and format for group process and individual reflection

Cooperative learning will increase student achievement by as many as 28 percentile points (Darling, 1999).

Verbalization

Verbalization is the practice of encouraging the learner to express the learning and connection-making process to themselves and others through self-talk, voicing thoughts, discussion, thinking, and writing. Verbalization will enable learners to

- Visualize and verbalize new learning and connections, activate prior knowledge, and build new cognitive frameworks for new ideas, concepts, and principles
- Utilize the power of dual encoding (making connections as they "talk it out") to assimilate and conceptualize new information
- Communicate new learning through self-talk and/or discussion
- Explore and communicate ideas
- Develop an awareness of the way in which their minds work as they monitor their own mental activity (metacognition)

When encouraging verbalization, the teacher will

- Provide an environment that encourages students to voice thinking while monitoring the execution of complex tasks
- Enhance discourse by consistently providing opportunities that stimulate problem solving, question raising, formulation of conjecture, presentation of solutions, and determination of validity
- Encourage the use of self-talk, invented terms and symbols, analogies, metaphors, stories, written hypotheses, explanations, arguments, oral presentations and dramatizations, and metacognition to explore and share understanding of new concepts and ideas

Verbalization will increase student achievement by as many as 46 percentile points (Darling, 1999).

Engaged Learning

Engaged learning is a set of teacher practices that actually engage the student in the instruction that is taking place. Engaged learning will enable students to

- Move, manipulate ideas and representations, interact, and reflect on learning
- Spend more quality time on task
- Achieve a greater depth of knowledge regarding concepts, ideas, and principles being learned
- Construct meaning for the material or concepts and acquire deep meaning and understanding of the content to be learned
- Process new learning into long-term memory

When using engaged learning, the teacher will

- Prepare their instructional delivery to include relevant, worthwhile, and stimulating explorations for all learners
- Utilize participation as an assessment for engagement

- Integrate multiple learning styles to optimize engagement
- Monitor types of practice most successful for each student
- Organize space and schedule to maximize time on task and immersion into worthwhile hands-on activities, simulations, tasks, and activities that convey and embody new learning

Engaged learning will increase student achievement by as many as 31 percentile points (Darling, 1999). This strategy is an excellent one to accomplish what Benard refers to as providing opportunities for students to participate in the learning.

Differentiated Instruction

Differentiated instruction meets the diverse needs of students through flexible grouping, based on the adjustment of context, process, and content/product in response to student readiness, interests, and learning profiles. This strategy allows students to

- Set goals in partnership with the teacher, based on student readiness, interest, and learning profile
- Self-assess to maximize academic strengths and improve areas of weakness
- Explore and apply key concepts for the learning content at an appropriate instructional level
- Construct meaning from contextualized content that is culturally responsive
- Participate in groups that may be readiness-based, interest-based, constructed to match learning styles, or chosen to maximize specific multiple intelligences
- Experience success regardless of academic level
- Become a self-directed learner

When using differentiated instruction, the teacher will

- Act as a facilitator of instruction to guide students in goal setting
- Use flexible grouping to enable success for all learners across the spectrum, from struggling students who need to grasp and use new knowledge to advanced students who need to maximize their learning potential
- Use differentiated strategies (e.g., contextualized curriculum, culturally responsive strategies, anchoring activities, clustering objectives, contracting, compacting, tiered activities, centers, pre- and post-assessment, etc.)
- Design and deliver instruction with a multiple intelligence orientation
- Embed ongoing assessment into instruction, based on student growth and goal attainment, to monitor individual progress closely

Differentiated instruction will increase student achievement by as many as 34 percentile points (Darling, 1999).

Goal Setting

Goal setting is a strategy used to help students set specific, realistic, and measurable goals for learning. Goal setting will enable learners to

- Identify strategies and tools for organizing time and tasks so that proper resources will be used and the goals will be met
- Make choices about content, timing, work partners, project, process, environment, or resources that challenge the brain, are relevant to the learner, and engage the learner
- Increase intrinsic motivation because well-defined goals, chosen by the student, improve the learner's content beliefs and context beliefs and provide a clear purpose to the student for learning

When using goal setting, the teacher will

- Present strategies or heuristics for goal setting, provide an opportunity to practice, and give feedback to the student
- Help student develop a graphic representation of his or her goals in relation to the learning
- Provide practice by applying to real-life situations and content goals

Goal setting, an essential skill for all students, will increase achievement by as many as 40 percentile points (Darling, 1999).

Dr. Robert Brooks, a Harvard Medical School psychologist and author of *The Self Esteem Teacher* (1991), uses the attribution theory (which examines the explanations children offer for why they believe they succeed or fail at tasks) to explore locus of control, self-esteem, and resilience in children. Brooks believes that teachers have the capacity to be the person with whom children identify and from whom they gather strength to overcome adversity and hold on to hope. As with Vitto and Benard, Brooks stresses helping students to solve problems and engage in decision making. He also suggests that teachers help children look at problems as opportunities to learn rather than something that can defeat them. They do this by modeling how mistakes should be handled when they (the teachers) make them. He suggests that if teachers are to develop resiliency in children, it is critical that they help them develop a positive attitude toward making mistakes.

When teachers observe self-defeating behaviors, such as quitting, not trying, or acting like the class clown or class bully, they recognize ineffective coping strategies that cover up feelings of vulnerability, low self-esteem, and hopelessness. We need to help these students see what their strengths are, to make modifications so they can achieve using these strengths. Some of the modifications Brooks suggests are

- Giving untimed tests to lessen anxiety
- Defining a maximum time for homework. If most students in the class can do 10 problems in 30 minutes, then teachers can set 30 minutes as

the maximum time. If some students can only do 5 problems in 30 minutes, then their assignment should be 5 problems. The maximum time is set.

- Ensuring that students know what the homework assignments are by providing a list of assignments or an assignment buddy who ensures that the assignment is copied off the board accurately
- Allowing students to use computers for assignments when writing is difficult

When teachers use effective instructional strategies that provide meaningful opportunities for students to participate, they build resilience in students to succeed in spite of the obstacles they face in their lives.

In summary, we know that building resilience in students living in adverse conditions will ensure that these students succeed in spite of those conditions. To build resilience, turnaround teachers show caring and support, hold high expectations for every student, and provide opportunities for students to participate. Turnaround teachers apply the most effective instructional strategies to engage their students in constructing meaning of the content.

In the next two chapters, we discuss instructional strategies for you to use for the learning expectations, or state standards, that students must master, relative to the kinds of knowledge represented by those standards.

Teaching Declarative Knowledge 4

When we examine the cognitive system, we usually view it in terms of the declarative knowledge or procedural knowledge represented by the state standards that identify the learning expectations. Why? Declarative knowledge and procedural knowledge should be taught and assessed differently because they are stored and retrieved differently in the brain. Declarative knowledge involves the "what" or "what it is." It is the information about a concept or topic. Declarative knowledge might mean being able to remember a list of steps such as division steps (i.e., divide, multiply, subtract, bring down); facts, such as multiplication facts; concepts, such as civil rights; and vocabulary definitions, principles, ideas, understandings, and generalizations. Information (declarative knowledge), in order to be learned, must be stored in memory. We say our students have "learned" information when they can remember (recall, retrieve) it at will. We teach declarative knowledge differently than we teach procedural knowledge, and we assess it differently as well.

These are specific examples of declarative knowledge:

- Understands the concept of "freedom of speech"
- Knows the answer to 2×5
- Understands the properties and theorems of roots, exponents, and logarithms
- Understands that words and pictures convey ideas or meaning in a text
- Understands that animals have characteristics that help them adapt to their environment
- Knows the causes and effects of the American Revolution
- Knows the rules that govern various sports
- Understands the concept of "conservation"

Knowing how the student's brain learns information is critical in order to effectively teach declarative knowledge. In this chapter we examine multiple ways to teach declarative knowledge so that it can be remembered (stored in memory) and recalled for use later (retrieved), which will meet the needs of our diverse learners. We will also provide research-based strategies that are very effective in teaching declarative knowledge.

⧽ How the Brain Learns Information (Declarative Knowledge)

Declarative knowledge, or information, is primarily learned as a storage and retrieval function in the brain. Information is learned (stored *in* long-term memory) and must be remembered (retrieved *from* long-term memory) to be useful to the student. There are five pathways that we know the brain uses to store and retrieve information. However, most classrooms rely very heavily in their teaching on one pathway to memory—the semantic pathway. We can meet the learning needs of our students from poverty, our students from diverse cultures, and our English language learners by teaching information (declarative knowledge) through *multiple* pathways to memory rather than relying on the semantic pathway, which is the least reliable of the five pathways. It is how we modify our teaching of declarative knowledge to meet the unique needs of our learners that sends information to other pathways. According to Sprenger (1999) semantic memory relies on words, and it has to be stimulated by "associations, comparisons and similarities" (p. 51). English language learners and students who lack the vocabulary knowledge of the topic will struggle to store and retrieve information from this memory pathway. Let's examine how we can teach information to help our students to store and retrieve information (declarative knowledge) more effectively.

Semantic Memory

Semantic memory holds information from words, both auditory and visual (from print). This is a very difficult lane for learning because it takes so many repetitions to make it effective. Jensen (1997) reminds us that the semantic memory system that operates out of the cerebral cortex is not well designed to handle print and text information such as textbooks. In order to effectively utilize this memory pathway, students must be highly motivated to learn. Why? This pathway requires rehearsal, is isolated from context, and may lack meaning for the student.

When teachers use the semantic memory pathway, they should draw parallels to the students' experiences so that the chances of the association lasting longer are heightened. For example, if the teacher is teaching about the life cycles in grades 2 through 12, and plants are used as an example of the cycle, the type of plant used and the cultural experiences of the students will make a difference. If tulips are used, those children who have no experience with tulips will not associate them with the growing or life cycle. However, if the plant used for inner-city children is a geranium, there is a better chance of connecting to their prior knowledge. Thus to strengthen the use of semantic memory the teacher should use experiences that are relevant to the experiences of the students.

Episodic Memory

Episodic memory is the context, spatial, and location memory. This memory is more easily accessed because you are always somewhere as you learn something, so there is an association of the learning to a location (Sprenger, 1999).

When you walk back into a room hoping that the sight triggers what you forgot, you are trying to access episodic memory. There has been interesting research in which students are given math tests in an English classroom, or English tests in a math classroom, and the students consistently underperform. The theories behind the research results are that the context, or location, of the memory actually becomes part of the learning.

Some information is remembered, then, as it relates to a location. Have you ever driven down a street and immediately remembered something about it or that happened to you on it years ago? Episodic memory is context driven: Where did I learn the information, or where did I see or hear it (Tileston, 2004, 2009)?

Procedural Memory

Procedural memory is sometimes called "muscle memory." It is the memory pathway that is the combination of abilities we use when we drive a car, ride a bike, skip rope, or tie a shoe. Procedural memory stores the sequence of the processes that a body does. This is the memory lane that we use when we were learning to drive. When we are learning the process, we are very cognizant of each step: getting into the car, checking the mirrors, making sure it is in gear, and performing all the activities involved in driving the vehicle. While learning processes we are very aware of every movement involved in the activity, and then once they are learned they become automatic to us (Tileston, 2004, 2009).

Automatic Memory

Automatic memory is sometimes called conditioned response memory. When I hear the first note or two of those old high school songs, it's amazing how many of the words I automatically sing that I didn't know I remembered.

Other examples of automatic memory are the alphabet, multiplication tables, word decoding (but not comprehension), and reading music. Rhymes (i.e., jump rope, hand claps), rituals, hip hop sayings, pow-wow songs, and rapping are other examples that may be relevant to diverse learners.

Automatic memory can cause other memory lanes to open. You start singing the alphabet song, and your episodic memory is triggered when you remember your first grade classroom. You remember the name of your teacher, which opens the semantic lane, and swinging at the playground, which activates your procedural memory. You remember how happy (or scared) you felt that day, which activates your emotional memory. Children will also remember how sad or scared they felt that day because of a racial or sexist comment made about them or about their disability. This will also activate their emotional memory. That is why it is important to correct these incidences so that children remember that the adults addressed them fairly and consistently.

Remember our earlier example on learning to drive? Once we learn a process, so that it is automatic to us, it becomes a part of this memory system. We no longer have to think through each step of the process, but instead perform the process automatically.

Emotional Memory

The brain gives priority to emotions, so emotional memory takes precedence over every other type of memory. When emotion takes over, other memory lanes can be closed. The release of stress hormones can interrupt transmission and make clear thinking impossible. Logic can be lost and the memory lanes become inaccessible. The implications for teaching are sobering. Brain research indicates that students under stress, regardless of intent or motivation, can be physically unable to store memory or learn. A part of emotional memory that students who are diverse must deal with daily are the stresses of prejudice and stereotyping.

Ironically enough, strong emotion can also produce the strongest memories and learning, making it the most powerful type of memory. And emotional memory can activate the other memory lanes at the same intensity levels. When considering the diversity of the population in our schools and the characteristics of the five pathways, it is essential to remember that brain processes may be similar, but experience and context could be different. As we draw upon student experiences, teachers must not assume that the experiences are the same across all students. Consequently, it is important to have students share experiences and, as teachers, be knowledgeable about culture, linguistic, and economic experiences of a great variety of students.

How Can We Teach Through Each of These Pathways?

Using what you know about the five memory lanes makes it easier for you to plan lessons that use and incorporate the memory lanes that you intend. The most powerful teaching, of course, occurs when you are able to incorporate all five lanes into your lessons.

Semantic Pathway Memory Strategies

Remember that semantic memory operates word by word and needs to be processed in many ways because the brain has a hard time making the neural connections needed for semantic memory. Students use working semantic memory (rather than long-term memory) to get through tests or pass a course. The students didn't actually learn the material. They just found ways to keep it in semantic working memory long enough to write the answers down or complete their homework. Long-term learning is difficult with semantic memory. Have you ever had a student say to you on test day, "Hurry, hurry and give me the test before I forget"? They are just saying the answers over and over to themselves so that they can write it down and then promptly forget it. If you were to ask them the same question a week from now, they would not remember the answer. These students are merely holding the answers in short-term memory until they can write them on the test (Tileston, 2004, 2009).

Because of the word-by-word structure of semantic memory, material must be presented in short chunks of information, followed by some way of processing.

Strategies to Store Information

Graphic Organizers and Representations to Create a Mental Picture

Using graphic organizers is a superior teaching strategy to help students create and embed, or store, a mental picture of semantic information in long-term memory for later access or retrieval. The brain stores and retrieves pictures more easily than words. Graphic organizers help students to utilize "deep processing" to embed the learning into the brain. Graphic organizers are visual organizers and help organize information into a pattern to link new knowledge to prior knowledge.

Mental pictures, drawing pictures, and engaging students in kinesthetic activity can be successfully used as graphic organizers.

Mnemonic Devices

Mnemonic devices can be an enjoyable way to put very simple information into semantic and automatic memory. Acronyms, the first initials of the words you want to remember, are easy to remember. In fact, most of us can recall the colors of the rainbow that we learned in first or second grade because of Mr. ROY G. BIV. Acrostics, the first initials of each word in a sequence, also translate into long-term memory easily. Remember the music staff? EGBDF, "Every Good Boy Does Fine." Mnemonic devices work for both storage and retrieval but are not useable for concepts, principles, or generalizations. Develop acronyms that are culturally diverse for your students.

Repetition

Content material repeated enough times becomes a procedure. The brain stores procedures for easy access in the cerebellum. This strategy works well with students of color and with adolescents. Hip-hop music is full of repetitions that can be used to assist students in learning new material.

Chunking

Chunking is a process through which the brain perceives several bits of information as a single item. The brain can handle seven "bits" of information at a time. After that, it needs to "chunk" those bits together by classifying them. The classification label then becomes a new "bit" of information. Words are common examples of chunks. The more items put into a chunk, the more information processed in working memory and remembered at one time.

Students need to be coached in the process of chunking. It is a learned skill best taught procedurally. Use relevant experiences and problems to teach chunking. Students who are diverse use chunking in speech, music, and play.

Summarizing

Summarizing can be either student directed or teacher directed. Repetitions of concise summary statements help students cement the material in the semantic memory lane. Summarizing with peers helps students retrieve semantic memory by providing the opportunity for students to "fill in the blanks" with background knowledge.

Encourage a short or one-sentence summary. Make it a silly, pseudo-competition, going down the row to see who can come up with the most concise summary.

Role-Playing

Breaking the students into cooperative groups helps to keep role-playing fresh and interesting. In high school English, role-play what could happen next in the text. In social studies, role-play scenes from history, such as during the bubonic plague, the Crusades, the Trail of Tears, the Japanese internment, the Underground Railroad, or the lettuce boycott. Because semantic memory must be stimulated by associations, comparisons, and similarities, role-playing activities help students store and retrieve semantic memory by activating episodic and emotional memory lanes.

Peer Teaching

Peer teaching helps students develop interpersonal skills and evaluation and synthesis skills to develop higher-order thinking skills. Peer discussion and repetition of the content during the discussion help embed semantic memory. When students are allowed to participate across gender and culture, it allows for students to have positive experiences with people different from themselves.

Debates

Whether discussing capital punishment, the causes of World War II, the establishment of Indian reservations, mandating English only in public schools, or the detention system at their school, debating is an excellent way for students to examine and analyze semantic information. When students need to find proof, or facts, for their arguments, they critically read and discuss, problem-solve, draw on prior knowledge, and use emotion to cement semantic information into memory.

Outlining

Traditional outlining is an alternative to graphic organizers. Placing students in groups of two or three make the process more enjoyable, and the ensuing discussions of pro and con, compare and contrast, or other problem-solving strategies used to create the outline help to activate prior knowledge. Semantics are organized, put into a pattern, and repeated, which all contribute to moving semantic memory into long-term storage. Outlining is an effective strategy to store semantic memory as well as to retrieve semantic memory. Offer students the choice of traditional, longitudinal circle, or web forms of outlining.

Strategies to Retrieve Information

Advance Organizers

One type of graphic organizer that helps learners retrieve background knowledge is called an advance organizer. This type of organizer is used by the teacher prior to content instruction to activate previous knowledge, focus attention during instruction, and organize new information as it is being presented.

Advance organizers enable students to retrieve relevant background knowledge and past experiences related to the new content that will be introduced. Examples of the many ways advance organizers may be used include K-W-L charts, prediction trees, planning trees, concept webs, and anticipatory guides.

Brainstorming

Brainstorming, which is usually used as a cooperative or group activity in which a large number of words or ideas are produced in a very short amount of time, is an effective technique to retrieve information.

Students generate a number of possibilities, based on prior or background knowledge, and do not restrict their responses by judging the quality of the response before they answer. All possibilities are included, whether or not the idea or possibility is relevant, realistic, appropriate, or applicable. Let students know that they should refrain from making comments until the brainstorming session is complete. This includes nonverbal cues. Time becomes an element that is culture specific. American Indian and some Asian and Somalian students will think before speaking, whereas African American, Latino, or European American students will call out a response immediately.

Concept mapping is a graphic organizer on which concepts, ideas, people, things, places, and so on are mapped. This follows a brain-friendly pattern, as the brain seems to like and respond to patterns. Following is a list of various types of maps that are variations of the concept map.

Semantic Mapping

One of the most effective techniques used to help students retrieve information from prior knowledge, and for giving teachers a picture of students' schemata, is semantic mapping. Although it was developed for use in language arts, it can be adapted for use in any subject area.

Semantic mapping can be used to initiate students' thinking about what information they already know so that the teacher can make connections between the new ideas that will be addressed and the students' existing knowledge. New thinking and knowledge can build on what is already there. Prior knowledge information can be expanded, broadened, enriched, deepened, modified, changed, rearranged, corrected, or adapted.

The semantic map is an arrangement of words that indicate semantic meaning around a topic. Relationship words, attribute words, phrases, concepts, or any other combinations that indicate semantic meaning can be utilized. When a semantic map is constructed, it becomes a vehicle to connect new knowledge to known knowledge.

Anticipation Guide

An anticipation guide is a teacher-generated series of statements about a topic that students respond to before the lesson in order to retrieve prior knowledge. Students make predictions about the lesson content by using prior knowledge and ideas. At the end of the lesson, student responses are reviewed to produce an understanding of the new material presented after the lesson is complete.

Previewing

Previewing gives students the opportunity to retrieve information before the lesson begins. Students determine the purpose and relevance of the lesson and generate questions about what they want to know.

Think-Pair-Share

In this activity, students generate what they know (background knowledge) about the content matter being presented. They then pair up with another student and share their prior knowledge. The pairing should include crosses of gender, race, culture, language, and socioeconomic backgrounds. Sometimes it is OK to pair based on the similarities of students. It is best to have a balance, however, so that students get practice working with both students similar to them and students that are different.

Cues and Questioning Prompts

Cues and questions are ways to help students use what they already know about a topic. While the two techniques are similar, they differ in that cues involve a preview about what the students will experience. Cues are straightforward ways of activating prior knowledge or retrieving information.

Techniques utilizing cues and questions account for as much as 80% of what happens in a classroom on a given day. To be effective, cues and questions must focus on what is known and what is important versus what is unusual, which is commonly focused on in many classrooms. To properly cue and question a culturally diverse group of students, it is important to know information about their cultures. Often cues are culturally specific and, consequently, if consideration is not given to the diversity of backgrounds, the process may leave out some students. If the cues given cover more than one culture, or at least the cultures represented in the classroom, then the students will more likely feel that they are included. Questions that require learners to analyze information, rather than just recall or recognize information, produce more learning. The difference is that higher order questioning techniques require students to apply their knowledge in some way. Yet much of the classroom questioning has tended to focus on answers that do not require critical thinking skills.

Questions should be asked before a learning experience to introduce the topic and retrieve prior information. Many teachers have a tendency to think of questioning as a technique to use after the learning activity, thereby missing the opportunity to use questioning to jump-start the lesson.

Using open-ended questioning and having the students make up the questions to stimulate prior knowledge are two effective ways of using questioning to trigger semantic memory. This technique is very effective with diverse learners. Be sure to include oral as well as written questions. When students talk, listen, and think through possible answers, they retrieve prior information and process semantic learning. As students formulate questions, they begin to comprehend material at higher cognitive levels. The acts of questioning and making connections between different ideas help students retain new ideas and concepts. However, there appears to be some dissonance across cultures on the use of questioning techniques. Communication styles vary. For example, some American Indians are brought up to show respect for people of knowledge and authority by not asking direct questions. The communication style of direct questioning may not be effective with students raised in cultures with this value. To retrieve prior knowledge in such situations a teacher may use another strategy. Instead of the teacher asking the direct question "How many dinosaurs were in the picture?" The teacher may say, "Tell me how many dinosaurs you saw near the trees in the picture."

During a lesson, the teacher may direct students to write questions in the margin in order to react to a statement, concept, or theory. Students can be asked to jot down feelings, opinions, or questions in the margin. Based on newly forming questions and thoughts, students will make connections to prior knowledge of information based on newly learned facts and concepts.

☒ Episodic Memory Pathway Strategies

Strategies to Store Information

Field Trips

Take field trips and short excursions to make the content more meaningful. Making the learning more unique may make the learning more permanent. While field trips are typically content driven (a unit on animals means a trip to the zoo; a unit on drunk driving includes a trip to the courthouse), field trips of that magnitude are obviously not practical to include in your lessons on a daily basis. Move outside on a sunny day, work in the library, or bring your ninth-grade class to sit in a circle in the kindergarten room. Think of anything you can to make the learning unique, especially when the material is challenging. Field trips help embed or store episodic memory about the experience. Field trips also allow students who are bodily/kinesthetically intelligent to thrive. Most learning is done sitting down and with pencil and paper. Using field trips helps students who are physically active by providing structured movement.

Room Arrangement

Changing the arrangement of the desks in your room to make your room unique or rearranging the groups of students after each unit or topic can help your students make better use of the episodic lane. Sitting in the same desk place can confuse information across units.

However, a caution is in order here. Moving students around also strips them of their episodic memory. Think through changes before you apply them to be sure you are actually providing more opportunities for new episodic learning and not inadvertently erasing existing memories. It's a good idea to not change the student placement until the end of a unit, end of a topic, or after the assessments have been completed for a unit or section of material.

Strategies to Retrieve Information

Color Coding

Use one color of paper for each category of handout you use. As you are retrieving information, ask them to think about or remember the "blue sheets" or the "yellow sheets." Make sure that none of the students are colorblind or have trouble seeing colors that are not red or green.

Color has cultural significance. Use colors that are positive symbols for your students:

African American/African descent	Red, black, and green
Chinese	Red
Swedish	Yellow and blue
Polish	Red and white
Irish	Green or orange

Bulletin Boards

Bulletin boards are used liberally for elementary aged students but less so as the students move up into higher grades. Bulletin boards are an excellent trigger for episodic memory and brighten up any room from preschool through college-aged students.

Use bright colors for your bulletin board unit and provide a model, if appropriate. Use pictures, posters, symbols, examples, slogans, and other eye-catching graphics. Make sure the bulletin boards depict males and females in nontraditional roles, those who are disabled, as well as different family structures (i.e., single mother, single father, two parent, two parent/same gender, disabled parent, etc.). If your bulletin boards have more than one language, students begin to identify with linguistic diversity, and students who speak or read the language feel included.

Junior high and high school math classes can include symbols, formulas, and sample problems for the unit on their bulletin boards. The boards can also display the origins of the particular type of math or science as well as cultural-based math games. Science classes can include the key elements of the periodic table, classifications of animals that are valued by various cultures, or a historical time line from varying cultural perspectives (i.e., Africa—the rise and fall of civilizations, American Indian—invasion of their indigenous lands, Mexican/Latino—e.g., loss of parts of Mexico). Social studies units on Europe or Africa could highlight history, contributions, or crops and then compare and contrast from a U.S. perspective and from a European or African perspective.

Area Teaching

During each unit of study, teach from a consistent place in the room. Your location will help them associate episodic memory of the content taught. As students work to recall information and activate their prior knowledge about a content item, teach them to ask themselves, "Where was the teacher standing?" This assists them in activating the episodic memory lane. Wait until you start a new unit before you vary your location. Changing location at the same time a new unit begins adds novelty for the brain to attend better and provides a "clean slate" for new episodic memory.

Wear hats, masks, or other decorations and costumes that illustrate the unit. Make sure that the costumes are not the traditional dress of cultural groups of people. If traditional dress is used, then it should be called traditional dress, not a costume. Using the term *costume* could be interpreted as an insult, as costumes are generally worn during Halloween or at masquerade parties. If you make it fun, colorful, and interesting, students will remember.

Procedural Pathway Memory Strategies

Strategies to Store Information

Repeat Performance

Repeated performance of a procedure continues to be the most effective way of stimulating procedural memory. When a process is repeated over and over, the brain stores the process in the cerebellum for easy access. The difficulty is that the process must be repeated enough times to be accessed in long-term memory. Doing one science experiment, trying one long jump, riding a bike once—these processes do not become procedures if they are not repeated many times within a fairly short time period.

Manipulatives

Hands-on techniques, such as Cuisenaire rods for math, tangrams, or mancala games, help develop conceptual understanding and problem-solving strategies.

Invented Procedures

Anything that provides movement offers the opportunity of producing procedural memory. Jump, clap your hands, have the students clap with you. Have the students listen for key words that they need to respond to by jumping out of their desks. A favorite advanced geometry teacher did a handstand each time students brought up a connection to Euclid, his favorite mathematician, or to his favorite number, 5, which represented the five basic rules of geometry as well as Euclid's May 5 (5/5) birthday.

Puppets, shadow boxes, marching, and games are not only for the younger grades. Older students love "regressing"! If you are teaching challenging content, ask your students to stand when they "get it," shout "hallelujah," bow from the waist, or give a high five. Adding movement and fun has a huge impact on creating long-term memory.

Strategies to Retrieve Information

Manipulatives

Hands-on techniques help students retrieve stored information by cueing the sequence of actions that comprised the procedure. An eleventh-grade chemistry student, for instance, might have difficulty remembering how to prepare slides for the microscope, even though the student prepared slides in biology in tenth grade. Physically handling the slides and microscope, or starting the physical sequence of fine motor steps, activates the student's prior knowledge by "kick-starting" the sequence of steps.

Movement

Retrieving procedural memory can also be accessed by starting with the first few steps of the procedure. Riding a bike, skipping, playing jacks, playing soccer, and water skiing are all examples of activities that can be recalled (retrieved) many years after being used.

Automatic Pathway Memory Strategies

Strategies to Store Information

Music

Rap, poems, and other types of rhythm and music devices are guaranteed strategies. Virtually anything can be put to music or a beat, and virtually every student can learn (store) or remember (retrieve) almost anything with rhythm and music.

Students can write their own songs, or they can rewrite the words to existing melodies. Songs are easy to remember, can be practiced repeatedly, and can be used in many contexts. Younger children can learn math facts, multiplication tables, or the list of prepositions set to music.

Repetitions

Other automatic strategies are repetitions and drills. Flashcards, quiz shows, and other repeated oral work in math, social studies, science, and English produce automatic learning.

Strategies to Retrieve Information

Music

Music can be effective as a retrieval procedure: hearing only one or two notes can trigger an incredible amount of detailed memories. Older students can use music and rhythm to help learn the 50 states, the periodic science table, American Indian reservations in a state, the countries that have Spanish as their official language, and math mnemonics.

There is some research that indicates that music is especially effective to improve math storage and retrieval, perhaps because both utilize patterns and symbols.

For your diverse learners, music is effective if it is the music of the students. Some music will not be motivating to some cultural groups or age groups. If students know that you are going to play a variety of music, then they will not be turned off. It is important that the teacher ask students what music they like and use it, as well as other music. Teachers should also vary the music by introducing different cultural music, making sure that the cultures in the class are represented.

Emotional Pathway Memory Strategies

Strategies to Store Information

Create the Emotions

Create emotions in your classroom. Set up a scene and include the emotional climate of the content area. If you teach science, set up the excitement of winning the Nobel Prize or finding a cure for polio. In history, divide the class in two, and make one side the Allied powers and the other side the Axis powers, or assign pro- and anti-war camps for the Vietnam War. In English literature, study the emotions of the characters, and role-play the most dramatic. Share your likes and dislikes (within reason) and passions for your subject and the content.

Celebrations

Celebrate, debate, and find other cooperative activities that engage the entire class in emotion. Celebrate what they've done well with surprise celebrations as well as planned ones. Celebrate both the beginning and end of a unit to add to the emotional memory. Add music, and write songs to commemorate the learning occasions. Use well-known melodies, and let the students' creativity go wild.

Music

Music itself is strongly emotional. It can be dramatic, funny, sad, speculative, searching, angry, dynamic, or loving. In your classroom, play songs appropriate for the content, such as "Yankee Doodle" during your study of the American Revolution, to harness the students' emotional memory. Use music as background music to set the tone for the content that you are teaching. Use somber, brooding music as a background to a unit on Pearl Harbor and Japanese music for a unit on the Japanese internment. Use a television theme for a humorous connection, such as the theme from *The Pink Panther*, before a math project. In each case be sure that the humorous connection is not one that puts down women, other countries, or groups of people, even subtly. Use music for no particular connection at all, other than to connect the learning in a powerful pathway. Use music of many cultures to engage all of your students.

Strategies to Retrieve Information

Use Emotions

Start by activating prior knowledge about the information. What do your students know about this topic? How do they feel about the topic? Elicit humor, if possible, to provide a relaxed, positive emotional climate for your students.

Research-Based Instructional Strategies for Declarative Knowledge—Information

As you examine the following research-based strategies for teaching information, or declarative knowledge, be mindful of how you can utilize multiple pathways to memory to help students to store that information so that it can be learned and retrieved later at will.

Vocabulary Strategies

Teaching vocabulary is critical for students of poverty who come to school with half the vocabulary of their middle-class counterparts. It is also critical for our students who are learning English. Vocabulary is the lowest level of declarative knowledge, but it is the building block upon which all other levels of declarative knowledge are constructed. Students cannot express their background knowledge without the vocabulary to do so.

Cultures vary in the amount of information that is explicitly transmitted through verbal language versus the amount of information transmitted through context, relationship, and physical cues. Cultures that are high on use of context rely less on words than learning through shared experience, history, and implicit messages. Asian, American Indian, Arab, Latino, and African American are examples of high-context cultures in which meaning comes from communications other than solely through the use of words. Carroll (2001) described the communication of these particular cultures by stating that "facial expressions, tensions, movements, speed of interaction, location of the interaction, and other subtle 'vibes' are likely to be perceived by and have more meaning for people from high-context cultures." People of low-context cultures (e.g., European Americans) may not process gestures, environmental clues, and unarticulated moods that are core to effective communication in high-context cultures. Examples of low-context cultures are Anglo-European American, Swiss, German, and Scandinavian. Their style is highly verbal linguistic, precise, direct, and logical (Carroll, 2001).

Marzano, Pickering, and Pollock (2001) provide an excellent strategy for teaching vocabulary in a five-step process that also meets the needs of diverse learners.

Step 1: The teacher provides a definition or description of the term or vocabulary word.

Step 2: The teacher provides a nonlinguistic (few, if any words used) organizer to show the meaning of the word.

Step 3: The student creates a definition of the term in his or her own words.

Step 4: The student creates a nonlinguistic organizer that represents the critical attributes of the term.

Step 5: The student periodically reviews his or her nonlinguistic organizer to add additional detail as he or she learns more about the word.

This process uses more than the semantic pathway to memory to learn vocabulary. Think about ways you could enhance this process using other pathways to store the information about a vocabulary word.

Explicitly teaching vocabulary will make as many as 49 percentile-point gains in achievement (Darling, 1999). For students of poverty, English language learners, and students of color, preteaching the vocabulary prior to the beginning of a lesson or unit will help to level the playing field so that they can actively participate in making meaning of the content from which the vocabulary was drawn.

Semantic Mapping

One of the most effective ways to teach vocabulary is through semantic mapping. Using this tool will increase achievement by as many as 49 percentile points (Darling, 1999). Semantic mapping is defined by Allen (2004), based on the work of Stahl and Clark (1987) and Heimlich and Pittleman (1986), as "a teacher-directed study of a word or concept in relation to other related words and ideas" (2004, p. 17). To teach the concept, graphic organizers or maps are used to help students visualize their thinking. A mind map is one of the ways that semantic mapping might be demonstrated. Another type of map that we like is the attribute wheel. If we want students to not only know the definitions of genres such as fantasy, tall tale, and myth but also to know why a tall tale is not the same as a fantasy or a myth, this is a great tool. An attribute wheel is an example of semantic mapping that helps students use what they already know and build on that knowledge to gain understanding. The following steps are involved in using an attribute wheel:

1. Provide a simple definition of *attribute* to your students and explain how you will be using the attribute wheel.

2. Provide students with an attribute wheel frame.

3. Ask them to place what they already know on the spokes of the wheel.

4. Discuss the attributes that they have listed, being sure to clarify any misconceptions.

5. Together, add other attributes until you have enough attributes that define the word well.

Concept Attainment

Concept attainment is a process for discovering the identifying characteristics and discriminating attributes of a concept, principle, generalization, or idea and for reflecting on how the learning occurred.

Concept attainment will enable learners to

- Learn the critical, distinguishing attributes of a concept, principle, or generalization
- Provide examples and nonexamples of a concept to demonstrate understanding
- State the rule for inclusion/exclusion to demonstrate understanding of the defining rules for that concept
- Process how they learned the concepts, principles, and generalizations in order to embed the new knowledge into long-term memory by connecting it with prior knowledge

Teachers using concept attainment will

- Act as a recorder, keeping track of the hypotheses and the identifying characteristics and attributes
- Prompt and focus the thinking, and supply additional examples as needed during the process
- Choose when to best apply the strategy whether at the beginning of a lesson to introduce the distinguishing characteristics, in the middle as a check for understanding, or at the end as a powerful evaluation of the depth of learning

Graphic Representations

Graphic representations are visual organizers used as a way of giving information a pattern for better understanding and meaning making, such as semantic maps, Venn diagrams, T charts for comparing and contrasting, and so on.

Graphic representations will enable learners to

- Represent and organize main ideas and key concepts, vocabulary, causal relations, symbols, concepts, principles, and generalizations
- Represent the connections between new information and known information
- Process the learning of that information into long-term memory

Teachers using graphic representations will

- Prepare and teach the graphic organizer or representational framework
- Prompt students on the content being represented or organized, such as relationships between pieces of information (main idea and supporting detail), hierarchical structure, patterns, and so on

Graphic representations will make as many as 49 percentile-point gains in achievement (Darling, 1999). It is a powerful tool for use with declarative information.

Explicit Instruction

Explicit instruction is a teacher-directed activity that includes methods such as lecture, didactic questioning, explicit teaching, drill and practice, demonstrations to learn specific information, and step-by-step sequences with specific forms of practice. It is an effective tool for declarative knowledge if, and only if, the levels of practice are attended to diligently. Using this strategy with diverse learners requires teachers to make a concerted effort to explore ways to add pathways to memory besides the semantic pathway. Otherwise, it is ineffective.

Explicit instruction will enable learners to

- Learn concepts, lists of steps, and information
- Utilize three levels of practice: controlled practice, guided practice, and independent practice, moving from one level to the next based on demonstrated mastery
- Use graphic organizers to represent information
- Achieve content mastery and mastery over learning rules and steps required for application of the content

Teachers using explicit instruction will

- Orient the students to the new information by activating prior knowledge
- Explicitly teach new information using effective presentation skills
- Direct students to test their grasp of the information by using the three forms of practice until specific learning criteria have been met
- Provide explicit feedback and reinforcement

Explicit instruction, used appropriately, will make as many as 49 percentile-point gains in achievement (Darling, 1999).

⧩ Summary

Declarative knowledge involves the information from the standards to be learned. It is a prerequisite to learning procedural knowledge. Declarative knowledge involves rules, tactics, generalizations, principles, concepts, vocabulary, and facts. It is easy to teach, but it is very difficult to learn. The semantic memory system, which is the pathway we generally use to teach information, is the least reliable of the memory systems and requires a connector if it is to be easily recalled by students.

There are five pathways to memory that can be used to teach information so that students can learn (store) information and remember (retrieve) it at will. Besides the semantic pathway, there are the episodic, procedural, automatic, and emotional pathways. Teaching so that students can use multiple pathways to store information dramatically increases the chances for students of poverty, students from diverse cultures, and English language learners to remember (retrieve) it.

Vocabulary is the building block for all declarative knowledge or information. Preteaching vocabulary utilizing multiple pathways to memory will allow diverse learners to participate in the applications of subject matter content and level the playing field. Students need adequate vocabulary to express their prior knowledge and thoughts about the subjects that you teach.

Once your students have the information relevant to your content standards, they are ready to construct meaning of that content through applying it. They cannot demonstrate applications of your subject matter content without knowing and/or understanding the information (declarative knowledge) first. The next chapter addresses how teachers assist their students in applying the information to make personal meaning of the content.

Teaching Procedural Knowledge (or Process) 5

W e know that declarative knowledge is the *information* that we want students to know. It is the easiest to teach and the easiest to test. The world of work requires that we be able to do something with that information. When we ask students to demonstrate their learning

- by applying the information;
- by comparing information;
- by analyzing information;
- by categorizing information;
- by drawing conclusions about information;
- by writing about information;
- by synthesizing information;
- by evaluating information;
- by debating about information;
- by creating new information;
- by making inferences about information;
- by making decisions about information;
- by solving problems with information; and
- by hypothesizing about information and so forth

we are asking them to demonstrate what they can do with information—the processes and skills of procedural knowledge. In this chapter, we discuss what procedural knowledge is, how the brain learns so that it can ultimately make meaning through those processes, how we can differentiate to meet the needs of students from poverty and diverse cultures, and finally the most effective, research-based instructional strategies to use at every step of the way to teach procedural knowledge.

An easy example of learning procedural knowledge that most of us have experienced is the process of getting a driver's license. The first part of the process was to learn the rules of the road, the meanings of the signs on the road, and, for some of us, the parts of the car that we needed to know about. During this process, we read a book and memorized the speed limits for residential roads, the meaning of the sign indicating that traffic merges, and the rules for passing another car. We took a written test on that *information* (declarative knowledge).

Did we then get our driver's license? No. We had to *demonstrate* a set of skills. We had to parallel park, we had to demonstrate that we could follow the traffic signs, and, for some of us, we had to demonstrate that we could get the manual transmission car moving without grinding the gears and getting off to a jerking start. Only after we had passed a behind-the-wheel test of demonstrating our skills (procedural knowledge) were we issued our driver's license.

Procedural knowledge is more difficult to teach and test. Yet we know that it is the most important to be learned.

How the Brain Learns Process

In order to better understand how to teach procedural knowledge, it is helpful to understand what happens in the student's brain in response to the presentation of any learning task. We will use Marzano's systems of thinking (1998), which is divided into three stages that the brain goes through in learning. All learning proceeds through these three stages.

First Stage—Self System—Do I Want To?

When teachers initially present their students with a learning task (e.g., distinguishing between fact and fiction, understanding the process of photosynthesis, comparing and contrasting democracy versus communism and socialism, estimating distance in feet and inches, writing a persuasive paper, etc.), the student's brain first engages the self system.

When the self system of the brain is engaged, the student asks,

- Do I want to do this?
- How important is this to *me?*
- Do I believe I can learn this task?

The significance for students from poverty and diverse cultures is that they are more likely to answer, "No." Why? The learning tasks presented by most teachers have not been made relevant to the diverse cultures in the classroom, nor are they relevant to what is important to students living in poverty. In addition, students from poverty and diverse cultures are more likely to have had negative experiences with past learning; consequently, they lack the self-efficacy to believe that they can be successful. During engagement with the self system, the brain is concerned with *motivation* and *volition* and *relevancy*—do I want to, is it relevant to me, and am I motivated to learn this task?

If students of poverty and diverse cultures determine the answers to be *no*, learning does not occur.

Second Stage—Metacognitive System—How Will I Do It?

Let's assume that the teacher has presented a learning task, the self system has been engaged, and the student wants to begin the learning task, is motivated to learn, and believes he or she can learn. The metacognitive system is then engaged. The student's brain then asks,

- What are my goals?
- How will I learn best?
- What strategies do I need to use to achieve my goals?
- How will I monitor my learning so I know I'm achieving my goals?

If students cannot set a goal to accomplish the learning task, don't know how they learn best, don't have any strategies from their past to call upon, and have no way to monitor their learning along the way, the students will be overwhelmed, and very little learning will occur. A sense of hopelessness sets in, and children quit and sometimes announce, "This is too hard! I can't do it." Or they blame the learning task itself. You may have heard in your classroom, "This (task) is so dumb! Why do we have to do this?" These are defense mechanisms used by children who don't know how to set goals, plan, and execute that plan to accomplish the task.

The metacognitive system in the brain contains information about the nature and importance of the plans, timelines, resources, and strategies for accomplishing the goal. Many of our students from poverty don't have experiences with planning or with the processes they need to follow through on a plan. Children from generational poverty, or students living in areas of concentrated poverty, live more in the here and now, which doesn't require planning. In schools, we typically expect the planning, setting timelines, finding resources, and identifying strategies for accomplishing a task to be done independently. Our children from diverse cultures are more successful if this is a collaborative rather than independent activity.

Third Stage—Cognitive System— What Will Be My Approach to Make Meaning of the Content in This Task?

The cognitive system is responsible for the *effective processing* of information that is necessary for learning. You might ask, "If the cognitive system is where the *processing* occurs, why do we, as teachers, need to know about the self system and the metacognitive system?" The answer is because you cannot get your students to engage in effective processing if they disengage in the process before their brain gets to this stage.

Again, all learning proceeds from the self system to the metacognitive system and only then moves to the cognitive system. That means that all students' brains begin by engaging the self system regardless of where we begin the lesson. If we start class by going right to the substance of the lesson, students may miss part of the information while they are going through the process of deciding if the information is personally relevant, whether they want to pay attention, and so on. That is why we recommend that teachers attend to the self system and the metacognitive system.

For example, let's say we've presented our students with a learning task, and they've successfully engaged both the self system and the metacognitive system. The cognitive system asks,

- What learning strategies do I know for this task?
- What parts of this task do I already know how to do?
- How is this task similar or different from another task I know?
- What information do I need to learn?
- What skills do I need to learn and refine?

When the cognitive system is engaged, it interacts with the knowledge domains: declarative knowledge (information) and procedural knowledge (skills and processes). Almost every state standard, goal, and objective of the expected learning for students is found in the knowledge domains. If the cognitive system remains successfully engaged, students will be successful in learning.

Why Do We Need to Differentiate Instruction for Processes?

As much as we care about our students, we cannot change the conditions under which our children live. Those conditions might include poverty, languages that *we* are unable to speak, cultures and values that are different from our own and that *we* don't understand, violence, homelessness, drugs, or any other number of things.

What we *can* do is use the most effective, research-based instruction, modify it to meet the needs of diverse learners, and provide the conditions in school that will ensure that all children can achieve and succeed. That kind of teaching is called differentiated instruction for diverse learners, and it will allow all children to achieve, and it will close the gap in achievement among groups of children. Differentiating instruction will require a shift in beliefs, perspectives, and practices that begins with us, as teachers.

Teachers everywhere have tried to differentiate instruction to meet the needs of the children in their classrooms. Their attempts are framed by their own "set of glasses," or perspectives about human development and about how schooling ought to happen. Most teachers in America have a "set of glasses" from a European-American cultural value system and were raised in a middle-class environment. From that perspective, or set of glasses, teachers have done an incredible job of meeting the needs of white, middle-class children to learn and succeed. They share the same culture and background experience, which provides the lens by which they communicate expectations, rules, norms, beliefs, appropriate behaviors, and assumptions about "normal" human development and learning.

Williams (2003) states, "All learners come to formal education with a range of prior knowledge, skills, beliefs, and concepts that significantly influence what they notice about the environment and how they organize and interpret it" (p. 5). This is the influence of *culture*—which is the lens through which we learn and develop our set of glasses.

The consequences of not attending to culture when differentiating instruction for learning procedural knowledge—where students make meaning of the content—can be seen in the recently released 2007 STAR test results shared by California state superintendent of public instruction, Jack O'Connell. We learned that even when poverty is *not* a factor, the performance of black and Latino students is behind those of white children (Mangaliman, 2007, p. 1). California's STAR tests results show that African Americans and Latinos who are not poor perform at lower levels in math than white students who are poor. Jack O'Connell notes that "these are not just economic gaps. They are racial achievement gaps." We as teachers must address culture and build resilience in children by differentiating instruction to meet the needs of all of our students so that all can achieve. This is critical when we are trying to teach procedural knowledge where a student makes meaning of the content she focuses her attention on, how she interprets the world to make meaning, what background knowledge she brings to the learning, and how she will value learning. As the National Task Force on Minority High Achievement and current assessment data from state tests show, minority students (with the exception of Asian Americans)—even those who are *not poor*—tend to score lower on achievement tests than whites who are poor (Manning & Kovach, 2003). Culture trumps poverty in its impact on achievement and on the achievement gaps between students. If we are going to effectively deal with the issues of poverty, we must first deal with the individual differences of our students based on their culture through differentiation.

※ What Are the Implications for Teaching Procedural Knowledge?

When teaching procedural knowledge to students living in poverty and from diverse cultures, we need to address three issues to ensure that all students will make meaning through the processes learned (procedural knowledge):

1. Providing culturally responsive teaching

2. Delivering the instruction in an environment that will foster resilience (high expectations, opportunities to engage in learning, caring and support)

3. Using strategies that are proven to make a difference in engaging students from the self system to the metacognitive system to the cognitive system for procedural knowledge

Culturally Responsive Teaching

Teaching in a culturally responsive manner requires that we broaden our set of glasses to learn about the cultures represented by our students (Gay, 2000, 2002; Villegas, 1991). Culturally responsive classrooms have two critical attributes: the inclusion of students' languages, cultures, and daily experiences into both the academic and social context of school, and the explicit teaching of the dominant culture's expectations of schooling so that all children can fully participate (Zeichner, 2003). This means that we have to build a bridge between the culture of the school and that of the home or community.

To create a culturally responsive classroom requires that we help students find a way to work collaboratively toward a goal. The goal is using, developing, and constructing knowledge and requires the practice of five major principles (Shade, Kelly, & Oberg, 1997). The culturally responsive classroom is the context in which procedural knowledge can be taught.

Principle 1: A learning community must be inviting.

Principle 2: The leader of the learning community must send personally inviting messages.

Principle 3: An inviting classroom has firm, consistent, and loving control.

Principle 4: An inviting learning community provides students with a sense that they can accomplish the tasks being asked of them. It enhances and fosters good academic self-concept.

Principle 5: An inviting learning community stresses collectivity rather than individualism.

In an inviting classroom the environment makes students feel at home and that they are contributing members. The physical and psychological environment welcomes students. They know how to function within this environment and know that the classroom will satisfy their basic needs. The desks are placed to enhance interpersonal relationships between the teacher and the students, as well as among students.

When the teachers send personally inviting messages, they indicate that they are caring, accessible, and dedicated. This is evidenced in their facial expressions, their dress, and their persona. Students sense that they are special and important to the teacher. Verbal and nonverbal messages indicate that they hold high expectations for all of their students. They communicate patience, understanding, enthusiasm, and flexibility in creating an environment for teaching and learning. They inspire their students and produce a sense of self-worth and pride of achievement in their students. Teachers have power!

The classroom that is managed with firm, consistent, and loving control eliminates the conflict between home and school. Sometimes there is a fear that if teachers give up an inch of control, they will lose total control of the classroom and chaos will reign. This fear is often based on a lack of knowledge about the culture of the students in their classroom. Shade et al. (1997) state, "The differential use of discipline creates the most cultural conflict as social control mechanisms used by teachers of culturally different students are significantly different from those used by the students' parents" (p. 51). To effectively manage students from poverty and diverse cultures, we should address misbehavior privately, not single out or reprimand students in front of the group. We need to be sure to separate our response to misbehavior from our response to the child. If these students perceive a withdrawal of caring because of misbehavior, they feel rejected, and there's a perception of inordinate cruelty.

When teachers are communicating to students that they can accomplish the tasks before them, they are creating a positive academic self-concept. Children from poverty and diverse cultures often come to school with a self-concept in all areas but academic self-concept (Shade et al., 1997). They often come to school with perceptions of inferiority. Sometimes achievement in school represents the loss of one's ethnic identity and is perceived as "acting white." Teachers need to mirror the assets of students back to them; this communicates to children that their teachers are aware of potential that the students themselves might not be aware of. An inviting classroom that honors the cultures from which students come does not make students choose between the dominant culture and that of home. Teachers will communicate their belief that their students can achieve, that they expect them to achieve, and that they will not give up on them—no matter what!

By respecting the need for collective action rather than stressing individualistic or competitive social interaction, we can eliminate some of the conflict. The family or peer group is often more important than the individual in many cultures. Triandis (1990), in his work on motivation, observed that the emphasis on individualism versus collectivism is probably the most important cultural difference in social behavior that can be identified. This is because it determines whether children will pursue and value their own individual goals over those of their tribes, family, work groups, and fellow group members to achieve their own goals, or whether they will place the collective goals ahead of their own. Providing students from poverty and diverse cultures opportunities to work collaboratively (e.g., cooperative learning, pairs, study buddies, etc.) honors their collective or group value system. We should be mindful that 70% of the world's population lives in a collective culture. The values exhibited by this culture are reciprocity, obligation, duty, tradition, dependence, harmony, and an emphasis on family integrity and interdependence. By both paying close attention to the culture of the school and incorporating important cultural elements of the children, the school becomes comfortable to both students and teachers and results in increased academic achievement—the goal of a culturally responsive classroom.

Creating an Environment That Will Foster Resilience

In Chapter 3, we addressed why developing resilience is so important. When teaching procedural knowledge so that children can make meaning of the content we are teaching, we need to remember to listen to their stories, to show caring through individual attention, and to respect and honor the cultural assets they bring to school. We create an environment that will foster resilience in which meaning making can flourish when we have a "no excuses" message that communicates high expectations. We give them a voice and a chance to actively participate in the learning in culturally meaningful ways.

One example of this is the use of the African American *griot* to begin and end the day. This is a call-and-response strategy that permeates learning in the African American community and is accomplished in a variety of ways.

GRIOT: Greetings, Brothers and Sisters.

CLASS: Greetings, Griot. (Group claps three times.)

GRIOT: Today's affirmation is, "I have solved problems like this before."

CLASS: (Individual students interpret what the affirmation means to them and for the work they must do for the day. They also relate how the affirmation will help them to be successful in their respective tasks.)

GRIOT: The Griot is finished.

CLASS: Thank you, Griot. (Group claps three times.)

Use Strategies That Are Proven to Make a Difference in Engaging Students in Meaning Making (Procedural Knowledge)

In teaching the processes and skills of procedural knowledge so that children of poverty and diverse culture can make meaning, we want to choose strategies that make a significant impact on academic achievement, modify them for diverse learners, and address all of the stages of thinking that the brain uses in learning. The following strategies are drawn from the Learning Bridges Aligned Instructional Database (Darling, 1999) for their impact on learning procedural knowledge. While it is not the purpose of this book to teach how to perform each strategy, we provide information on what each strategy will enable students to learn and those activities that describe the role of the teacher in delivering them. We provide the impact on academic achievement based on the research from which the strategies were placed into the Aligned Instructional Database.

Self-System Strategies

Activating Prior Knowledge

Activating prior knowledge uses storage and retrieval procedures (such as anticipation guides and KWL plus) delivered at the beginning of a lesson that are designed to elicit preconceived ideas, retrieve known knowledge and experience, and provide a focus for the new information.

Activating prior knowledge will enable learners to

- Activate and build on their prior knowledge and natural curiosity to learn more
- Restructure the learning task to connect it to a real life example in their experience (i.e., twins, weather, lottery tickets)

- Utilize concept maps, graphic outlines, and advance organizers to record the results of retrieved information
- Focus on the understanding that some events are more likely to happen than others and make connections for this understanding to what they already know

When using activating prior knowledge, the teacher will

- Identify the concepts that students will encounter
- Prepare nonlinguistic organizers to show that some events are more likely to happen than others (i.e., for making and confirming predictions, evaluating new information and hypotheses by testing them against known information, and drawing inferences, conclusions, or generalizations)
- Guide students in summarizing retrieved knowledge
- Assist students in representing the connections between the new and known information in a nonlinguistic representation

Activating prior knowledge will increase student learning by 46 percentile points (Darling, 1999).

Teaching for Relevance

This strategy was addressed in Chapter 3. It can be used to engage the self system so that the student will see why the learning is important to them. Perhaps a real life example of a teacher using this strategy will provide more insight.

Dawne Spangler taught the following lesson in her math class. Used with explicit permission of Dawne Spangler and drawn from the Learning Bridges course she authored by the same name, this story illustrates how students can learn procedural knowledge when relevance is provided.

Our guest speaker, Officer P. J. Janik has arrived and is chatting casually in the back of the room with my aide, Lorraine. Students wander in and seat themselves; the morning bell rings. P. J. and Lorraine are puzzled, because I have not arrived . . . unusual. Lorraine takes roll as P. J. begins his guest lecture on using mathematics in police work. The intercom interrupts—"There has been an accident. Will Officer Janik please meet the principal in the parking lot immediately!" P. J. says to the students, "Grab your calculators and follow me!"

Outside, students find my pickup truck stopped precariously on the ramp to the back door. Cones are in place, and police tape outlines a crime zone. A huge stuffed bear is wedged under the tires, and a long line of skid marks trails behind the truck. I am on my knees, crying over the squashed bear. P. J. takes charge of the "accident scene." He and the students must determine how fast the truck was going when I stepped on the brakes. Because this is a school zone, even a speed of 25 mph will be criminal speed, and I will be arrested for bear slaughter. P. J. rattles his handcuffs ominously.

(Continued)

(Continued)

We're off! In order to determine the speed of the truck, students must measure the skid marks left by each of the four tires, average them, and substitute that number into a complicated mathematical formula. This is a critical case, my freedom being at stake, and P. J. feels that the kids should practice first. He brings around the D.A.R.E. car, a vintage Corvette "donated" to the program by a convicted drug dealer. P. J. drives the car past the students, slams on the brakes, and comes to a stop. One set of students uses a radar gun to measure the speed, and another set rushes out with a trundle wheel to measure skid marks and use the formula. The two results are very close. However, P. J. tells us that the formula produces the most accurate measurement and is more credible in court. The experiment is run several times before all students are ready to investigate the crime. In fact, we collected data all day, through six classes of math students—accelerated, grade-level, remedial, and special education—before we reached a conclusion.

What happened?

1. We had a blast, and *no one* asked me why they needed to know this.

2. Students used formulas to solve real-world problems. This is included in the school curriculum, the state standards, and the NCTM standards. Each student practiced the algorithm many times.

3. Students transferred their understanding to other formulas commonly practiced in math classes (i.e., converting Celsius to Fahrenheit, simple interest, the quadratic formula, etc.). This transfer was demonstrated in various assessments.

4. Students saw P. J. in a different light, as someone who wanted to help them, who was approachable and friendly (his primary objective in participating in the exercise.) They also saw him as a guy who drives a Corvette!

5. Students learned that even slow-moving cars skid a long way before they stop. A car traveling 80 mph will skid 302 ft, provided that it doesn't spin, swerve, or flip. We paced it off to ensure that it was a concrete rather than abstract bit of knowledge.

6. Students learned that police officers can figure out what happened in an accident and are not distracted by "unclear memories" of witnesses. (One kid commented that he figured lying to a cop would only make you look even dumber.)

This lesson took exactly the same amount of time that I would have used to teach the objective in the book and cost exactly nothing.

The purpose of the exercise was to eliminate the traditional approach to this lesson (repeated practice of various formulas to get kids confident in their use—a worksheet) in favor of a recontextualization of the concept. Formulas are never used in real life unless there is a concrete goal in sight. We provided the students with a concrete goal. We structured the lesson to allow students to use kinesthetic intelligence, along with visual/spatial, interpersonal, and logical mathematical intelligence to make meaning from the lesson. With contextualized learning and kinesthetic activities, this lesson was inclusive of our urban learners, students of poverty, and culturally diverse students. Our cognitive learning environment was a parking lot . . . the Corvette was just an attention getter— pretty effective! (Spangler, 2001)

Metacognitive System Strategies

Verbalization

Verbalization is the practice of encouraging learners to express the learning and connection-making process to themselves and others through self-talk, voicing thoughts, discussion, thinking, and writing about what is being experienced in the learning process. More information on this strategy is provided in Chapter 3. This strategy can also be used to allow students in collaborative groups to plan together, identify priorities together, to "think aloud" together, and to voice their thinking processes with each other. With its superior impact on academic achievement, support of students from a collectivist value system, and provision of an excellent means to engage the brain's metacognitive system, this strategy is a must to use. Most teachers just need a simple reminder to put this strategy into practice.

Goal Setting

Goal setting learning is another powerful strategy used to help students set specific, realistic, and measurable goals for learning. It was also addressed more thoroughly in Chapter 3. It is a significant metacognitive system strategy and should be explicitly taught to students from poverty and diverse cultures.

Cognitive System Strategies

Academic Controversy

Academic controversy is a teaching practice in which the students take sides on an issue or opinion and present their case to the class. Prior to the student presentations, the teacher directly instructs on the criteria for presenting an argument successfully. Students choose a side and research it so that they present a clear and research-based argument.

Academic controversy results in increased achievement and retention, higher quality problem solving and decision making, more creative insight, more thorough exchange of expertise, greater task involvement, more positive interpersonal relationships, and greater social competence.

Academic controversy will enable learners to

- Research and prepare the best case possible for the assigned position
- Make a persuasive presentation

- Engage in an open discussion
- Refute the opposing position
- Rebut attacks on position
- Reverse perspectives
- Synthesize the issue

When using academic controversy, the teacher will

- Act as a guide to introduce the students to materials, help them to formulate positions, synthesize facts into issues, take positions, identify appropriate patterns of argumentation, refine and qualify positions, and test assumptions
- Use direct instruction initially to teach skills necessary to process and then transition to a student-directed presentation and discussion
- Provide source documents to students
- Facilitate positive and appropriate group process

Academic controversy will increase student achievement by 37 percentile points (Darling, 1999).

Group Problem Solving

Group problem solving is a strategy that involves student participation in small groups to maximize learning in the process of problem solving. The problem-solving process is utilized by the group while being internalized by the individuals within the group. Group problem solving will enable learners to

- Work in groups to formulate a prediction
- Communicate with each other and help one another with predicting a solution, discussing possible approaches, and constructing, demonstrating, and using the process developed by the group to solve a problem
- Show individual and group accountability by taking responsibility for their personal contribution, individual learning, and whole-group performance
- Develop appropriate social skills for working with others
- Reflect on individual contributions and achievement within the group
- Monitor and evaluate group process for problem solving whether or not a "correct" answer was given

When using group problem solving, the teacher will

- Model and guide how to think critically and how to work collaboratively
- Compose groups, furnish resources, and structure tasks so that individual accountability and group interdependence are both necessary
- Ensure that the process and product is intrinsically interesting
- Provide a resource-rich, positive, and safe environment for students to achieve individual and group goals

- Facilitate and encourage the positive and productive interaction
- Help students adapt and/or clarify their shared and individual goals
- Provide the time and format for group process and individual reflection

Group problem solving will increase achievement by 27 percentile points (Darling, 1999).

Jurisprudential Inquiry

Jurisprudential inquiry, using Socratic dialogue and case studies, is a process in which students negotiate legitimate differences and resolve issues on social policy that emphasizes our social nature, how we learn social behavior, and how social interaction can enhance academic learning.

Jurisprudential inquiry will enable learners to

- Use case studies as a way of negotiating, based on the belief that society has people who legitimately differ and conflict in their views, priorities, and social values
- Use Socratic dialogue as a way of contradicting students' general statements
- Demonstrate how to consider the motives, credibility, and perspectives of the others in their case studies
- Think about social policy (with conflicting motives, views, priorities, and values) and resolve controversial issues by successfully negotiating differences
- Apply the process and skills to conflicts in their own lives after they become competent in the use of the strategy, which is a powerful application of analysis, synthesis, and evaluation

When using jurisprudential inquiry, the teacher will

- Introduce the students to case materials, help them to formulate positions, synthesize facts into policy issues, take positions, identify appropriate patterns of argumentation, refine and qualify positions, and test assumptions
- Use direct instruction initially to teach analysis and argumentation and then transition to a student-directed discussion
- Provide source documents to students

Jurisprudential inquiry will increase student learning by 38 percentile points (Darling, 1999).

Teaching for Transfer

Teaching for transfer is the ability to learn in one situation and then use this learning in a modified or generalized form in other situations. Transfer of learning is the core of problem solving, creative thinking, and all other higher mental processes, inventions, and artistic products. Teaching for transfer will enable learners to

- Use prior knowledge to build on and expand new knowledge
- Expand critical thinking abilities
- Apply and combine basic principles to create new ways of thinking
- Internalize and incorporate the learning as personally relevant

When using teaching for transfer, the teacher will

- Present opportunities for students to identify prior learning that could assist in learning
- Assist students in identifying the effect that the prior learning has on the processing of new learning
- Guide the student in identifying the ways and the degree to which the new learning will be useful to the learner in the future

Teaching for transfer will increase student achievement by 37 percentile points (Darling, 1999).

Heuristics

Heuristics are the general rules, as opposed to a set of rigid steps, for processes such as decision making, experimental inquiry, reading, speaking, writing, problem solving, and investigation that students apply and practice with attention to how they might be improved. Teaching heuristics will enable learners to

- Identify similarities and differences, generate inferences about new knowledge, and use organizing ideas
- Comprehend material presented in written or oral forms (reading, listening, speaking)
- Present information in written form
- Make decisions, solve problems, perform investigations, and engage in experimental inquiry

When teaching heuristics, the teacher will

- Identify the heuristics that apply
- Use an advanced organizer to represent the general rules to students
- Provide opportunities for students to apply and practice with attention to how they might be improved
- Provide specific feedback to students

Heuristics will increase student achievement by 38 percentile points (Darling, 1999).

Self-Directed Inquiry

Self-directed inquiry requires an activity structure, which gradually requires the learner to assume responsibility for the learning of content at a higher level of understanding. Self-directed inquiry will enable learners to

- Decide upon a strategy to use in the learning process
- Verbalize the reasons behind the chosen approach
- Select more appropriate strategies, based on teacher feedback
- Use self-questioning techniques as a new problem is presented
- Assume responsibility and become self-sufficient in the learning process

When using self-directed inquiry, the teacher will

- Observe student approaches to a learning task
- Ask students to explain their approach to learning
- Describe and model a more effective procedure for accomplishing the task
- Provide new and similar learning opportunities, decreasing the teacher's role
- Check results by asking students to share specific learning strategies used

Self-directed inquiry will increase student performance by 37 percentile points (Darling, 1999).

Self-Evaluation of Learning

Self-evaluation of learning enables students to evaluate their own answers and responses. It provides cues, questions, and hints that call attention to appropriate responses. Self-evaluation of learning will enable learners to

- Reflect upon the answers and responses given
- Use partially correct answers as a basis for more accurate ones
- Develop higher cognitive levels of learning as answers are more fully developed
- Develop a level of generalization with various skills and content areas

When using self-evaluation of learning, the teacher will

- Allow students to reflect upon answers and responses given with regard to the learning task
- Provide cues, questions, and hints to foster in-depth thinking processes
- Give specific feedback as students revise answers and responses
- Encourage students to compare the original with revised responses

Self-evaluation of learning will increase student performance by 37 percentile points (Darling, 1999).

In summary, we have learned that procedural knowledge is comprised of the processes and skills that are used to demonstrate learning. When students engage in these processes and skills, they make meaning of the content represented by the learning expectations. In order to best achieve learning of these processes, as teachers we must use effective strategies to engage the brain's self system so that students will be motivated to learn. We must also explicitly teach them effective strategies that impact the metacognitive system so that they can plan, adhere to timelines, identify resources, and monitor their learning as they progress. We must use the most powerful strategies for teaching procedural knowledge from the cognitive system where students will make meaning of the content. All of this is embedded into a context that reflects cultural responsiveness and an environment that will foster resilience. Then we will have differentiated instruction to teach procedural knowledge to increase academic achievement and to close the achievement gaps between groups.

The Role of Leadership in the Poverty School

6

The role of leadership in the high poverty school is first and foremost to ensure that every student has access to a high-quality education. Those of you in positions of leadership know that the task is far greater and complex than it sounds. Equity to a high level of learning requires that the entire staff has received high-quality training on the instructional and emotional practices that make the most difference in student learning modified for culture and poverty. It requires that the resources of the community and the school system be fully utilized and that the mission of the school be steeped in understanding and determination where culture and poverty are concerned.

All too often, schools that teach in high poverty areas are in older buildings, have fewer resources, and have the teachers with the least experience. A study by Education Trust (2008) points to the disparities in the education of poor and minority children in contrast to their more affluent counterparts. Some of the conflicts pointed out in this study include the following:

- The percentage of minority students in "high minority districts" is 83.67%, as opposed to 3.3% in low minority districts. Thus we still have schools that are segregated by a variety of minorities, who are often also poor.
- While progress has been made in some states, others have slid backward, the result of which is that "our nation consistently spends fewer dollars educating students in its highest-poverty and highest-minority schools districts than it does districts with fewer of such students." (Education Trust, 2008, p. 4)
- While the number of English language learners (ELL) increases each year, inequity in spending exists in those states with a population of 10% or more ELLs. Texas and Nevada are cited as having the largest spending gaps, with each spending more than $1,000 per student less in high ELL districts.

- Nationwide the spending gap between high-poverty districts and low-poverty districts has widened from 1999 to 2005. In 1999, the gap between the highest and lowest poverty districts nationwide was –$848, and in 2005 that gap had widened to –$938.

The report also acknowledged that the biggest population growth in schools has been with ELLs. Using the estimates from Passel (2006), the projected growth of students needing ELL services is expected to move from 12 million in 2005 to 14 million by 2010 (Education Trust, 2008, pp. 4–5).

Schools still look at students in high poverty areas as needing to be "fixed" rather than asking how we need to change the educational system in order to better meet the needs of these students. Manning and Kovach (2003) say, "Clearly, the content of professional interactions remains largely focused on student- rather than curricular or systemic deficits" (p. 36).

Studies by Darling-Hammond (1997) and Kunjufu (2005) clearly show that a disproportionate number of black males are identified as "special education" students. We must come to realize that the system is broken for the 10 million children and counting who live below the poverty line. School leaders must demand better for our children.

School leaders must begin to demand better equipped facilities and resources for high poverty schools, and they must educate the public on why it is critical. It has been said that the only way that we change people is to change what they know. School leaders must become researchers with solid data to prove the need for equity for all students. The task is not one that involves only school leaders, but also every member of the staff, parents, the movers and shakers in the community, the ministerial alliances, professional organizations, and politicians. There is a need for social, religious, and governmental agencies that work with the poor to hold hands in an effort to not only educate these students but also to build resiliency.

What Leaders Do

Leaders not only lead but also delegate and know how to create learning communities—for their staff and for the people in their community. They know how to evaluate the resources available and how to prioritize needs. They know how to maximize their budget requests with solid data that shows what the need is and why it is crucial to students. They are always ready to answer why it is important for kids. For example, if the school traditionally receives teachers who are not fully certified or who lack the experience of the teachers sent to the more affluent areas, they know how to identify the kinds of training needed to make their staff highly trained, and they will settle for nothing less. Good leaders will seek the advice of various levels of the community, including students, parents, church officers, and those who have the ear of the community. While working in a high poverty area, we involved parents and community leaders through an advisory group called VIP (for "very important parents"). Those individuals were not necessarily the most educated or the most affluent in the community; they were the individuals who had the respect and the ear of other parents. They were often in the school and in the hallways, and they led in involving and keeping informed all parents in the community. We also had an advisory council of community leaders, ministers, students, teachers, and members of the VIP committee. At our first meeting, we asked, "If we could give you a better product, would you be able to pay for it in terms of tax dollars and in terms of your time and energy?" The answer was an overwhelming, "Yes!" The head of an industry within the community said that not only was he willing to pay for it in terms of tax dollars, but he would also be willing to release employees of his company to attend monthly advisory meetings with the school leadership.

Making Quality Learning Equitable

For decades education has struggled with how to make learning equitable. While *Brown v. Board of Education of Topeka* made equal access to education the law of the land, it fell short of doing the same for quality education. Society has paid the price for a system that has, on many levels, failed children of poverty and of color. In his book *Teaching Reading to Black Adolescent Males*, Alfred Tatum (2005) calls for schools to teach literacy on four levels. We have expanded his levels to include all cultures.

1. *Academic literacy.* We must provide scaffolding where it is needed to teach students how to learn. Scaffolding includes things like advance organizers, graphic organizers, vocabulary development, the heuristics needed to process information, and a clear rubric that provides the expectations in advance of the learning. Authentic methods of assessment that are directly tied to the objectives and the major premises of the learning are essential. Feedback should be provided often, and it should be both positive and prescriptive. In order to do this, educators must receive training on

- Brain research as it applies to learning
- Embedding culture into curriculum and instructional practices that reflect collectivist value systems
- Knowing and using effective, research-based instruction—the highest predictor of learning that exists
- Making technology an integral part of the teaching/learning experience
- Rethinking assessment
- Reframing high level thinking and creativity
- How to use collaboration more effectively
- Real-world applications to the learning
- 21st-century literacy skills
- How to make resiliency an everyday goal

2. *Cultural literacy.* The cultures of the classroom should be honored by all. Tacos on Tuesday is not cultural literacy. Where possible, the classroom, the books, the visuals, the learning styles, and the teaching methods should reflect the dominant culture of the classroom and honor all of the cultures. In order to accomplish this, educators must

- Know and understand the culture of the classroom and why it matters
- Understand and use collaborative learning appropriately
- Know the difference between collectivism and individualism and how culture affects each approach
- Honor the cultures within the classroom and school (and know how to do it effectively)
- Believe that all kids really can learn and learn at a high level

3. *Social literacy.* Tatum (2005) says that social literacy in the culturally diverse classroom is "the ability to navigate a variety of settings with people with similar or dissimilar views; being able to communicate in a variety of ways to achieve positive outcomes" (p. 35). Social literacy must be directly taught. In order to do this, educators must understand how to collaborate effectively in the classroom and how to integrate collaboration into the lessons.

4. *Emotional literacy.* Being emotionally literate means that we can control our emotions, our actions, and our reactions to others. It also means that we are resilient. When we build resiliency in our students from poverty, we provide them with a caring and supportive relationship, high expectations with no excuses, and opportunities to actively participate in learning to overcome adverse conditions and to be successful.

⫽ Training the Staff to Actively Engage Students

Louis and Ingram (2003) state, "In the majority of schools, teachers' lives focus almost exclusively on their classrooms. Hence, it is not surprising teachers prefer to work with the most responsive and quickest students—predominately those of the middle class and higher tracks" (p. 158). We talk about self-efficacy for our students; teachers also want and need self-efficacy in the teaching and learning experiences in the classroom. Teachers who experience failure often are probably not going to stay in the teaching field, or at least not in the high poverty areas where success is sometimes slower in coming. A strong leader who understands and is able to effectively use the research on working in high poverty areas can, along with his or her staff and community leaders, create a place where teacher commitment and engagement are high.

Louis and Ingram (2003, p. 159) list four types of engagement by teachers that are critical if students are to be engaged in the learning.

1. *Engagement with the school as a social unit.* You will know that your school has achieved this type of engagement when teachers love coming to work and when there is a sense of community in the classroom, in the teacher's lounge, and in the hallways. We have worked with schools in which the faculty barely know one another and where they may not even like each other very much. In these types of schools we always begin with team building and with helping the faculty determine why they are unhappy. One activity that we often use with faculties is to ask them to make a chart of all the things they dislike about their

job, the classroom, the learning environment, and so on. Once we have built the chart, we ask them to determine which of the items on the list they can control. We talk about constraints and blocks; these are very different.

2. *Engagement with students as unique, whole individuals rather than as "empty vessels to be filled."* In the culturally responsive classroom, relationships are built first and then the learning. Teachers know their students, and they know how their students learn best. There is a sense of belonging in the classroom, and students know it is OK not to know the answer, but it is not OK to not try. Several years ago, an experience with a young man from a gang made me realize how important this is. The young gang member said that the reason he joined a gang in the first place was to have a place to belong and a group to belong to. For some students the only place where they truly belong may be the classroom—it may be the only warm place in their lives. For seven or more hours each day we have the power to create a place where everyone belongs and where we are all learning together. Listen to your students and provide scaffolding so that they can be successful. Provide coaching, mentoring, and other forms of support when possible.

3. *Engagement with academic achievement.* We firmly believe in a staff development model grounded in strong research and in the learning communities model. In this model, all participants have common goals for the students they serve, and they are constantly learning. When we go to schools we are always amazed that so many of our schools are working from an antiquated framework. Education tools, like technology, are constantly changing and emerging. We know more now about the human brain than we ever have in the history of the world. We know that we learn our whole lives and that the plasticity of the brain is constantly changing. We know that the vast majority of students today are highly visual or visual/kinesthetic and that schools who rely on lecture alone are only teaching to about 10% of the students. We know that students who have had access to technology since a young age prefer to see the learning first and hear about it second. Yet the teaching model often employed with these students involves telling them first and then providing visuals (maybe) second. We know that teaching to every culture outside of the Anglo-Saxon background means that we must build a relationship with the students first and teach second. Yet the majority of schools are so pushed to "cover the material" that they teach first and, if time allows, build a relationship. When we began to use this model in our high poverty school, other school leaders said that we were setting ourselves up for failure, that we were wasting so much time on building relationships first that our state test scores were bound to come down; the opposite happened—test scores soared to 99% mastery in mathematics and 100% mastery in reading and writing. Did we mention that was in a high school? Scores in elementary and middle school came up even faster.

It took a strong commitment from school leaders to train a faculty not used to teaching high poverty students to learn which instructional strategies make the most difference and which modifications were important. That staff went through 14 days of training before they ever began to teach these high poverty students, and they received follow-up training periodically. Teachers were so zealous of the training they received that before new teachers were hired for that school, they were required to interview with present teachers from that school. It was understood that teachers seeking employment would not have had the same research-based training as the existing teachers, but the teaching staff wanted to make sure that the new teachers had the kind of belief system about poverty and culture that was essential to teach in that school.

4. *Engagement with a body of knowledge needed to carry out effective teaching.* Effective teachers know their subject matter and are constantly updating their knowledge base not only on their subject matter but also on pedagogy, brain research, and how best to reach their students. They participate in their professional organizations, and they are eager to participate in ongoing staff development. They make recommendations for the kinds of training they need, and they push for time to meet with their colleagues in learning communities.

How can education leaders know if the training provided to teachers and staff is well grounded? We recommend that leaders ask the following questions before employing anyone to train in their school or in online trainings.

1. From where does the research come?

2. Is there data available to show the effects of this training, this process, this method? A study in one school is not sufficient.

3. What kinds of credentials and background knowledge do the trainers or organization possess that make them experts in this field?

Remember that the instructional practices that work best with students from poverty and from a variety of cultures are based on the studies of instructional practices that have a high effect size with student learning in general. These instructional practices are then modified to meet the needs of diverse learners. They are modified based on the latest studies on cultures and poverty. Culture affects the way that students view learning, relationships, attitudes, values, and society in general. It is critical to know the culture of our students if we are to appropriately make the modifications needed for the learning to take place at an optimum level. Knowing about poverty and its effects helps us to determine what kinds of scaffolding or structures are needed for our students to learn.

Closing the Achievement Gaps 7

In the previous chapters, we have explored the critical impact that the learner's culture plays in learning, how we can create a culturally responsive environment that will foster motivation, the interventions we can use to build resiliency in our learners to succeed in spite of adverse conditions, the strategies and their modifications for teaching the declarative and procedural knowledge of each state's learning expectations, and, finally, the role of leadership in engaging parents and community to support the learners in school.

When we engage all of these components, we will have constructed a powerful new framework that will increase achievement and close the achievement gaps for diverse learning, that is, for students living in poverty, students from diverse cultures, and students whose primary language is something other than English.

Increasing Achievement and Closing Achievement Gaps

Teachers, schools, and districts do not have to choose between increasing achievement and closing the achievement gaps. It is not an either/or endeavor, but one of and/both. Improving achievement requires a focus on curriculum, instruction, and assessment. Closing the gaps in achievement for diverse learners means teaching that curriculum and providing a context for that curriculum based on the culture of the students in each classroom. It means using the best, most powerful instructional strategies drawn from the research and modifying those instructional strategies to meet the unique, cultural needs of the learner. It means using appropriate assessment for the kind of knowledge you are expecting students to learn and providing opportunities for students to use assessment as a tool for learning in a collectivist classroom respectful of their culture. Neither teachers nor students should have to choose.

When providing a context for curriculum that reflects the culture of students, teachers will use topics and teaching materials drawn from the rich sources of a multicultural world. These might reflect literature from various cultures, they may involve solving problems that pertain to their community, or they might be service projects that allow students to give something back to their communities. Students might use mathematics to solve real-life problems that are relevant to their lives. Contextualizing curriculum will increase the likelihood that students will engage the self system of the brain. They will be motivated to learn relevant content.

Teachers, using contextualized materials, will differentiate instruction by modifying the content, products, and process for making meaning for their students. Teachers who wish to increase achievement and close the achievement gaps will choose instructional practices that will yield the greatest learning for their students. However, they will modify those instructional practices to attend to the cultural differences their children bring. This may mean providing many and varied opportunities for students to work together collaboratively, respecting their collectivist value system. It might mean providing scaffolding for complex tasks until they can complete them independently. Teachers will want to provide opportunities for students to visually represent their thinking, relationships, planning, and learning with graphic representations. Students will be expected to attain mastery of the expected learning outcomes with clearly defined quality indicators. Terminology relevant to the learning will be pretaught to help level the playing field for students of poverty. We know that these youngsters come into kindergarten with only half of the vocabulary of their white, middle-class counterparts.

Although assessments given for final evaluations are often required to be individually completed, teachers will find ways to assist students to understand how assessments are created and approached in collaborative groups. This might be identifying the misconceptions that created wrong answers as a group. It might mean going through practice tests together. It might mean providing opportunities in small groups to examine questions and possible answers and thinking aloud to determine how assessments ought to be approached. Providing time for whole-class goals based on assessment results and cheering group goals also respects collectivist value systems.

Culturally relevant curriculum is driven by content standards that recognize the positive contributions of individuals and groups from diverse cultural, racial, ethnic, and linguistic backgrounds. It includes knowledge that reflects the culture of those in the classroom, school, and community in both images and texts. It aims to correct societal ills such as institutional racism, sexism, and classism both historically and in the present. It can affect self-concept, esteem, motivation, and resiliency of historically underachieving students (Ladson-Billings, 1995).

Culturally Responsive Environments

Classrooms that reflect the cultures in which students work and learn are viewed as welcoming places for learning to occur. In these classrooms, colors and the displays on the walls will reflect the cultures of the students. The seating arrangements for the room reflect opportunities for students to work together, to help one another, and to attend to the teacher.

Depending on the culture, there may need to be a place for movement in the classroom for cultures who learn that way. Teachers will provide collaborative opportunities for students to chorally read and respond so as not to single out anyone in the learning process. We encourage you to mentally stand on the threshold of your classroom and peek inside. If your student's culture is African American, how might your classroom look? If your student's culture is Hispanic, what would you include? If you have students from Vietnam, Iraq, Russia, or any other culture, what would you include?

Culturally responsive classrooms have a teacher who is personally inviting and welcoming. He or she listens attentively to students and shows personal attention to each student. The teacher is cognizant of eliminating any discriminating practices when calling on students. Some teachers actually keep track of who they have chosen to answer questions so they do not leave anyone out. The teacher will be aware of important values that each child brings to the classroom based on his or her culture and will respect them.

The teacher will help to distinguish between community materials and spaces that are shared, such as rulers, crayons, computers, and those that are private, such as individual desks or backpacks.

Classroom management will be firm, fair, and loving. Students will have an opportunity to share in the creation of the rules, rewards, and consequences. Teachers in a culturally responsive classroom work hard to distinguish between the child and his or her behavior. They will provide feedback on inappropriate behavior privately, not publicly. Teachers will praise for effort for group success even more than for individual achievement. A sense of community will prevail.

By creating a classroom environment that is culturally responsive to our students, we will create an environment that is conducive for learning for all of our students—those of poverty, those of diverse cultures, and English language learners. This will create the conditions where students are motivated to learn, believe that they can learn, and perceive learning to be personally relevant to them.

Culturally responsive instruction is driven by teaching standards that recognize the need to build upon the characteristics, learning styles, strengths, interests, and cultural background/heritage of the students in that classroom. It is based on the assumption that capitalizing on what students know, rather than just on what they do not know, is important. Culturally responsive instruction transforms curriculum content, learning content, classroom climate, student-teacher relationships, instructional techniques, and performance assessments (Gay, 2000).

Turnaround Teachers Build Resilience

Another critical component of a new framework needs to include turnaround teachers who build resilience in their students so that they succeed in spite of adverse conditions, whether those conditions be poverty, dysfunctional families, homelessness, drugs, violence, gang-infested neighborhoods, or any other number of things. Students should not be treated differently because of the circumstances in which they live. Turnaround teachers provide the conditions in school that will allow their students to succeed (Benard, 2003).

Turnaround teachers are caring and supportive, listen intently to their students, greet students at the doorway to make them feel welcomed, and show an interest in their students both personally and as students. They foster powerful relationships with their students, giving them hope when they may not have had any previous experience with that emotion. They encourage them to see a future beyond the here and now. These teachers help them to see obstacles as temporary and let students know that they believe they can overcome them. They mirror back the assets that they bring to the classroom (and that the students themselves may not be aware of and often are convinced that no one else has noticed).

These teachers hold high expectations for their students to succeed. They rise to the challenge of figuring out what each child needs to be successful and advocating for them to achieve. They accept no excuses for failure. There are many students for whom the reason they succeeded in spite of adverse conditions was a caring adult who believed in them so strongly that they could believe in themselves. Turnaround teachers will not let their students fail. They meet them where they are and provide the supports they need to succeed.

Turnaround teachers provide many opportunities for their students to actively participate in the learning experience. They provide ways for them to work together, to help each other, and to collaboratively work toward the classroom community goals. They provide as much choice as possible for students to determine how they will demonstrate learning. They provide opportunities for their students to lead. Rather than approach the learning process as one of passive receiving of information, they actively engage their students in the processes of learning so that they can construct meaning of the content for themselves.

Power of Early Childhood Intervention

We know that students of poverty often come through the door to kindergarten with a gap in achievement already in place (Karoly & Cannon, 2007). Klein and Knitzer (2006) document that, when done right, effective prekindergarten education helps narrow the achievement gap before children start school. A study conducted by RAND (2007) shows that children who attend effective early childhood programs perform better on standardized achievement tests in reading and math, are less likely to be identified as special education students, are less likely to be retained in school, and are more likely to graduate from school. Students of poverty do not have the background knowledge or the vocabulary of their middle-class counterparts. Early childhood intervention has been shown to increase the chances of children's being ready to learn in kindergarten. Yet the delivery of universal access to a high-quality early childhood program remains elusive. The children who lack access to quality preschool programs are disproportionately children of color, children whose home language is not English, and children whose parents did not graduate from high school. All children benefit from a high-quality prekindergarten experience.

In addition, teachers in early childhood programs are often the least prepared of all teachers and the poorest paid of all teachers. If we are to improve achievement and close the gaps for all students, teachers need to be provided with clear standards or foundations for developmentally appropriate learning expectations that interface with K–12 curriculums; with additional training in content, pedagogy, and child development in order to be able to teach the learning expectations; and an increase in pay to match that of teachers in the K–12 educational system. Quality early childhood programs are certainly the "ounce of prevention" especially needed by children of color, children living in poverty, and children whose families speak a language other than English.

※ Power of Professional Development to Widen Our Set of Glasses

If we are going to make a difference in closing the achievement gaps for diverse learners, we need to provide teachers with the professional development and support they need to learn how to deliver on the promises of this model.

In "The Funding Gap: Technical Appendix" (2008), Carmen Arroyo reports that teachers do not know what to do to help their children of color, their children of poverty, and their English language learners to succeed. The educational system's individualist set of glasses is what they have been taught to use in their classrooms. That set of glasses has worked extremely well for the students it was designed for—white, middle-class children. Unfortunately, the teachers with the least experience are most often those sent to high poverty and low performing schools.

Professional development needs to be provided to empower teachers to build culturally responsive classrooms, to teach them how to build resiliency in students so that they can succeed, and to guide them in differentiating curriculum for culture, modifying effective instruction for diverse learners, and learning how to attend to the processes—or meaning-making strategies—so that their students can achieve at high levels. They need to be provided information on how to learn about the cultures represented in the classrooms and in the communities in which their children live. They need to learn how to restructure their classroom management systems and the way students need to work together in order to learn.

Widening our set of glasses to include perspectives from the multicultural society that America has become will take time and additional training. It will require a change in how the key processes that define education are delivered. If teachers are to make that change, administrators and other education leaders need to take care of the teachers in the change process. Teachers need to be supported as they transition to a new way of teaching and as we create the structures to support the changes that are necessary to improve achievement and to close the achievement gaps. Teachers need to be supported with time, mentoring, and coaching in professional learning communities until the changes become institutionalized.

Teachers are already overwhelmed with the workload they carry. It is almost impossible for teachers to find the time and energy to take on "one more thing." Perhaps it is time that we explore a twelve-month contract for educators, with paid vacations and paid time for professional development, as is often seen in the business sector. If education is going to transition to a quality system that truly meets the needs of all of its learners in a timely manner, then the nation will need to step up to the plate to solve the time and funding problems equitably. We know what needs to be done. We need to find the will to do it. As it says on the sweatshirt, "Teaching is the profession that creates all others."

Leaders Engaging Parents and Community

If we are to truly look at the whole child, and not just the standards and benchmarks that prove what they have learned, we must find ways to join with community resources to provide for the needs of children. Nutrition, health—both mental and physical—spiritual nurturing, guidance, and support are necessary if we are to lift children out of poverty to become effective and successful members of society. If just teaching children were all it took, we would not have more than 35 million people living below the federal poverty line. For that matter, if just following the textbook and preparing for high stakes tests were the major components of education, we would not have gaps in learning. Teaching is a science, and we must look at all the variables if we want to know the results in advance. Principals must become instructional leaders who know how to get by not only with the entire staff but also with the community. The staff in high poverty areas must stand together to fight for better resources, high-quality teaching and learning, and a community and system that realizes it must provide for the mental needs of its children, as well as the physical, emotional, social, and health issues that must be tended. In this century the United States must prepare all of its children to be competitive in a global market, and that means that the responsibilities that were left to others in the past must be addressed by educators working with other organizations in the communities. The days of "it's not my job" are over.

Teacher Preparation

America has many colleges and universities that offer programs that license teachers. They are not graduating enough teachers fast enough to meet the number required. In order to fill the demand for teachers, many large, urban districts are seeking teachers from other countries or from programs that provide a fast-track approach to getting a teaching license. The teacher shortage is real, and it's escalating. Teachers leave the profession because they are not successful in the classroom. They are not prepared for the students they receive. The newest teachers are often placed in the lowest performing, highest poverty schools without any support for addressing the needs of their students from diverse cultures, those living in poverty, those living in constant violence, or those that are English language learners.

We suggest that even experienced teachers need ongoing professional development if we are going to improve achievement and close the achievement gaps. New teachers emerging from our existing postsecondary programs do not have the knowledge and skills to meet the needs of their diverse students either. They have been taught to teach in an education system that promotes an individualist value system designed for white, middle-class students. Given the demographic changes occurring in our society, those are often not the students in their classrooms.

Students emerging from four- to five-year education programs often have the knowledge of the subjects they teach. They have a few instructional strategies that they have been taught, but they don't know how to choose effective instruction for the declarative and procedural knowledge their students are expected to learn. They do not know how to modify that instruction for children living in poverty, those from diverse cultures, and English language learners. They do not know how to create a culturally responsive classroom or how to build resilience in students. They do not know how to contextualize curriculum or to use assessment as a means of learning. They do not know how to support students from a collectivist system of thinking.

Teacher preparation programs are beginning to "hold hands" with the districts and schools of the K–12 system, which is a powerful first step. They need to examine their programs and make the changes needed to deliver classroom teachers who know how to meet the needs of students in the 21st century, many of whom are not white or middle class. They need to follow these students and measure their effectiveness with all of their students in the classroom so that the teacher preparation programs, too, can continually improve the quality of teachers they graduate. Colleges and universities need to provide the knowledge and teach the skills that teachers require to meet the needs of students in a multicultural society, of students living in poverty, and students new to our country. Unfortunately, many states provide no incentive for knowledgeable teachers to work in high poverty areas. According to Arroyo (2008), "In 2005, districts serving the highest concentration of poor students received, on average, $938 less per pupil in state and local money than the lowest poverty districts, a gap that was essentially unchanged (given inflation) from 1999." In addition, this same report shows that teachers in high poverty areas tend to be paid less than their counterparts in low poverty areas.

Creating a Blueprint and Delivering On It—No Excuses

From California to North Carolina, state departments of education are focusing on creating blueprints for addressing the racial and poverty gaps in achievement. California's state superintendent, Jack O'Connell, appointed a P-16 Council charged with developing a plan for closing the achievement gap in California. Their report was delivered in January 2008 and included a three-phase plan to address the issue.

The issue of underachieving students is addressed in the strategic plans of almost every state we reviewed. North Carolina has held a statewide conference each year for more than a decade on raising achievement and closing the gaps. Most states' solutions continue to focus on efforts to improve achievement.

Solutions that will close the achievement gaps between groups need to focus on the learner and the culture through which the learner values education, focuses their attention, and makes meaning of the content presented to them.

Every state is charged with the responsibility to provide access to a high-quality educational experience for *every* student. There can be no excuses. Our quality of life, our economic growth, and our viability as a diverse, pluralist, and democratic society depend on it. It is within our reach if we have the will to act on it.

References

Allen, J. (2004). *Tools for teaching content literacy*. Portland, ME: Stenhouse.

Arroyo, C. G. (2008, January). The funding gap: Technical appendix. Retrieved November 5, 2008, from http://www2.edtrust.org/EdTrustPress+Room/fairshare2008.htm

Benard, B. (1996). Fostering resiliency in urban schools. In B. Williams (Ed.), *Closing the achievement gap: A vision for changing beliefs and practices* (pp. 96–119). Alexandria, VA: ASCD.

Benard, B. (2003). Turnaround teachers and schools. In B. Williams (Ed.), *Closing the achievement gap: A vision for changing beliefs and practices* (2nd ed., pp. 115–137). Alexandria, VA: ASCD.

Bomer, R., Dworin, J., May, L., & Simington, P. (2007). Miseducating teachers about the poor: A critical analysis of Ruby Payne's claims about poverty. *Teachers College Record, 110*(11). Retrieved September 6, 2007, from http://www.tcrecord.org. ID number 14591.

Brooks, R. (1991). *The self esteem teacher: Seeds of self esteem*. Loveland, OH: Treehaus Communications.

Brown, A., & DeLoache, J. (1990). Metacognitive skills. In K. Richardson & S. Sheldon (Eds.), *Cognitive development to adolescence* (pp. 139–50). East Sussex: Lawrence Erlbaum Associates.

Carroll, R. (2001). *Activating prior knowledge in Learning Bridges Online Professional Development System*. Chandler, AZ: Learning Bridges.

Cavanaugh, S. (2007). Poverty's effect on U.S. scores greater than for other nations. *Education Week, 22*(15), 13.

Cole, R. (Ed.). (1995). *Educating everybody's children*. Alexandria, VA: ASCD.

Csikszentmihalyi, M. (1990). *Flow: The psychology of optimal experience*. New York: Harper & Row.

Daniels, L. A. (Ed.). (2002). *The state of black America*. New York: National Urban League.

Darling, S. (1999). *Aligned instructional database*. Chandler, AZ: Learning Bridges.

Darling, S. (2008). *Model for differentiation based on culture and poverty*. Presented at Raising Achievement: Closing the Gap Conference, Greensboro, NC, April.

Darling-Hammond, L. (1997). *The right to learn: A blueprint for creating schools that work*. San Francisco, CA: Jossey-Bass.

Derry, S., Tookey, K., & Roth, B. (1993). *The effects of collaborative interaction and computer tool use on the problem-solving processes of lower-ability students*. (ERIC Document Reproduction Service No. ED374776)

Edmonds, R. (1986). Characteristics of effective schools. In U. Neisser (Ed.), *The school achievement of minority children: New perspectives* (pp. 93–104). Hillsdale, NJ: Lawrence Erlbaum Associates.

Education Trust. (2008, February 7). The funding gap. Retrieved February 14, 2008, from http://www2.edtrust.org/NR/rdonlyres/31D276EF-72E1-458A-8C71-E3D262A4C91E/0/FundingGap2005.pdf

The Freedom Writers with Erin Gruwell. (1999). *The freedom writers diary.* New York: Broadway Books.

Gay, G. (2000). *Culturally responsive teaching: Theory, research, and practice.* New York: Teachers College Press.

Gay, G. (2002). Preparing for culturally responsive teaching. *Journal of Teacher Education, 53*(2), 106–116.

Gilder, G. (1981). *Wealth and poverty.* New York: Basic Books.

Gorski, P. (2006). The classist underpinnings of Ruby Payne's framework. *Teachers College Record.* Retrieved June 9, 2007, from http://tcrecord.org. ID number 12322.

Gorski, P. (2008). The myth of the "culture of poverty." *Educational Leadership, 65*(7), 32–36.

Greenfield, P. M., & Cocking, R. R. (Eds.). (1994). *Cross-cultural roots of minority child development.* Hillsdale, NJ: Lawrence Erlbaum Associates.

Guskey, T. (2008). The rest of the story. *Educational Leadership, 65*(4), 28–35.

Guskey, T., & Gates, S. (1986). Synthesis of research on the effects of mastery learning in elementary and secondary classrooms. *Educational Leadership, 43*(8), 73–80.

Haberman, M. (1991). The pedagogy of poverty versus good teaching. *Phi Delta Kappan, 73,* 290–294.

Haberman, M. (1995). *Star teachers of children in poverty.* West Lafayette, IN: Kappa Delta Pi.

Haberman, M. (2005). *Star teachers: The ideology and best practice of effective teachers of diverse children and youth in poverty.* The Haberman Educational Foundation. Indianapolis, IN: Kappa Delta Pi.

Heimlich, J., & Pittleman, S. (1986). Semantic mapping: A heuristic for helping learning disabled students write reports. *The Reading Teacher, 40*(6), 506–512.

Henderson, N., & Milstein, M. (1996). *Resiliency in schools: Making it happen for students and educators.* Thousand Oaks, CA: Corwin.

Hernstein, R. J., & Murray, C. (1994). *The bell curve: Intelligence and class structure in American life.* New York: Free Press.

Hilliard, A. (1989). Teachers and cultural styles in a pluralistic society. *NEA Today, 7*(6), 65–69.

Jensen, E. (1997). *Completing the puzzle: The brain-compatible approach to learning.* Del Mar, CA: The Brain Store.

Johnson, W., Johnson, R., & Holubec, E. (1991). *Cooperation in the classroom.* Edina, MN: Interaction Book Company.

Karoly, L., & Cannon, J. (2007). *Who is ahead and who is behind?* Santa Monica, CA: RAND.

Klein, L., & Knitzer, J. (2006). *Effective preschool curricula and teaching strategies.* New York: National Center for Children in Poverty, Columbia University.

Kulik, C., Kulik, J., & Bangert-Drowns, R. (1990). Effectiveness of mastery learning programs: A meta-analysis. *Review of Educational Research, 60*(2), 265–299.

Kunjufu, J. (2005). *Keeping black boys out of special education.* Chicago: African American Images.

Ladson-Billings, G. (1995). Toward a theory of culturally relevant pedagogy. *American Education Research Journal, 3*(6), 465–491.

Louis, K. S., & Ingram, D. (2003). Schools that work for teachers and students. In B. Williams (Ed.), *Closing the achievement gap: A vision for changing beliefs and practices* (2nd ed., pp. 154–177). Alexandria, VA: ASCD.

Mangaliman, J. (2007). Poverty can't explain racial, ethnic divide. *Mercury News.* Retrieved August 16, 2007, from http://www.mercurynews.com

Manning, J. B., & Kovach, J. (2003). The continuing challenges of excellence and equity. In B. Williams (Ed.), *Closing the achievement gap: A vision for changing beliefs and practices* (2nd ed., pp. 10–36). Alexandria, VA: ASCD.

Markus, H. R., & Kitayama, S. (1991). Culture and the self: Implications for cognition, emotion, and motivation. *Psychological Review, 98*(2), 242–253.

Marzano, R. (1998). *A theory-based meta-analysis of research on instruction.* Aurora, CO: McREL.

Marzano, R., Pickering, D., & Pollock, J. (2001). *Classroom instruction that works: Research-based strategies for increasing achievement.* Alexandria, VA: ASCD.

Marzano, R. J., Kendall, J. S., & Gaddy, B. B. (1999). *Essential knowledge: The debate over what American students should know.* Aurora, CO: McREL.

McKinney, S., Flenner, C., Frazier, W., & Abrams, L. (2006). *Responding to the needs of at-risk students in poverty.* Retrieved January 18, 2008, from http://www.usca.edu/essays/v01172006/mckinney.pdf

McLaughlin, M., & Talbert, J. (1993). *Contexts that matter for teaching and learning.* Stanford, CA: Stanford University Press.

Merton, R. K. (1948). The self-fulfilling prophecy. *Antioch Review, 8,* 193–210.

Ng, J., & Rury, J. (2006). Poverty and education: A critical analysis of the Ruby Payne phenomenon. *Teachers College Record.* Retrieved October 14, 2006, from http://www.tcrecord.org. ID number 12596.

Osei-Kofi, N. (2005). Pathologizing the poor: A framework for understanding Ruby Payne's work. *Equity and Excellence, 38*(4), 367–375.

P-16 Council. (2008). Closing the achievement gap: Report of Superintendent Jack O'Connell's California P-16 Council. Sacramento, CA: California Department of Education. Retrieved January 12, 2008, from http://www.cde.ca.gov/eo/in/pc/

Passel, J. S. (2006). The size and characteristics of the unauthorized migrant population in the U.S.: Estimates based on the March 2005 current population survey. Pew Hispanic Center. Retrieved January 18, 2008, from http://pewhispanic.org/files/reports/61.pdf

Payne, R. (1998/2005). *A framework for understanding poverty* (4th ed.). Highlands, TX: RFT.

PBS. (1993). *Good morning, Mrs. Toliver* [Television series]. New York: Public Broadcasting System.

Peske, H., & Haycock, K. (2006). *Teaching inequality: How poor and minority teachers are shortchanged on teacher quality.* A report and recommendations by the Education Trust. Retrieved May 29, 2008, from http://www2.edtrust.org/NR/rdonlyres/010DBD9F-CED8-4D2B-9E0D-91B446746ED3/0/TQReportJune2006.pdf

Pink, D. H. (2005). *A whole new mind: Moving from the information age to the conceptual age.* New York: Riverhead Books.

RAND Corporation. (2007). Studies examine California's school readiness and student achievement gaps, and the state's system of publicly funded programs for preschool-age children. Retrieved March 8, 2008, from http://www.rand.org/news/press/2007/11/08/

Rank, M. R. (2005). *One nation, underprivileged: Why American poverty affects us all.* New York: Oxford University Press.

Rosenthal, R., and Jacobson, L. (1968). *Pygmalion in the classroom: Teacher expectation and pupils' intellectual development.* New York: Holt, Rinehart and Winston.

Rutter, M., Maughan, B., Mortimore, P., Ouston, J., & Smith, A. (1979). *Fifteen thousand hours.* Cambridge, MA: Harvard University Press.

Schwartz, J. (2000). *Fighting poverty with virtue: Moral reform and America's urban poor, 1825–2000.* Bloomington: Indiana University Press.

Shade, B., Kelly, C., & Oberg, M. (1997). *Creating culturally responsive classrooms.* Washington, DC: American Psychological Association.

Smith, M., & Wilhelm, J. (2002). *Reading don't fix no Chevys: Literacy in the lives of young men.* Portsmouth, NH: Heinemann.

Spangler, D. (2001). *Teaching for relevancy.* Chandler, AZ: Learning Bridges. Retrieved July 18, 2008, from http://www.learningbridges.com

Sprenger, M. (1999). *Learning and memory: The brain in action.* Alexandria, VA: ASCD.

Stahl, S., & Clark, C. (1987). The effects of participatory expectations in classroom discussion on the learning of science. *American Education Research Journal, 24,* 541–555.

Tatum, A. (2005). *Teaching reading to black adolescent males: Closing the achievement gap.* Portland, ME: Stenhouse.

Tileston, D. W. (2004). *What every teacher should know about learning, memory, and the brain.* Thousand Oaks, CA: Corwin.

Tileston, D. W. (2009). *What every teacher should know about learning, memory, and the brain* (2nd ed.). Thousand Oaks, CA: Corwin.

Tomlinson, C. (2008). Learning to love assessment. *Educational Leadership, 65*(4), 8–13.

Triandis, H. C. (1990). Cross-cultural studies of individualism and collectivism. In J. J. Berman (Ed.), *Culture, style and the educative process* (2nd ed., pp. 28–67). Springfield, IL: Charles C. Thomas.

Trumbull, E., Greenfield, P. M., and Quiroz, B. (2003). Cultural values in learning and education. In B. Williams (Ed.), *Closing the achievement gap: A vision for changing beliefs and practices* (2nd ed., pp. 67–98). Alexandria, VA: ASCD.

U.S. Department of Education, National Center for Education Statistics. (2007). *A profile of the American eighth grader: Student descriptive summary.* National Educational Longitudinal Study of 1988.

Valencia, R. (1997). Conceptualizing the notion of deficit thinking. In R. Valencia (Ed.), *The evolution of deficit thinking: Educational thought and practice* (pp. 114–179). London: Falmer.

Villegas, A. M. (1991). *Culturally responsive pedagogy for the 1990s and beyond.* Princeton, NJ: Education Testing Service.

Vitto, J. (2003). *Relationship-driven classroom management: Strategies that promote student motivation.* Thousand Oaks, CA: Corwin.

Vygotsky, L. (1990). The genesis of higher mental functions. In K. Richardson & S. Sheldon (Eds.), *Cognitive development to adolescence* (pp. 61–79). East Sussex: Lawrence Erlbaum Associates.

Wang, M. C., & Kovach, J. A. (1996). *Bridging the achievement gap in urban schools: Reducing educational segregation and advancing resilience-promoting strategies.* Alexandria, VA: ASCD.

Wang, M. C., & Reynolds, M. (1995). *Making a difference for students at risk: Trends and alternatives.* Thousand Oaks, CA: Corwin.

Waxman, H., Gray, J., & Padron, Y. (2003). Review of research on educational resilience. Scholarship Repository, University of California, Berkeley. Retrieved December 14, 2007, from http://repositories.cdlib.org/crede/rsrchrpts/rr.11

Waxman, H. C., Padron, Y. N., & Arnold, K. A. (2001). Effective instructional practices for students placed at risk of failure. In G. D. Borman, S. C. Stringfield, & R. E. Slavin (Eds.), *Title I: Compensatory education at the crossroads* (pp. 127–170). Mahwah, NJ: Lawrence Erlbaum Associates.

Wenglinsky, H. (2002, February 13). How schools matter: The link between teacher classroom practices and student academic performance. *Education Policy Analysis Archives, 10*(12). Retrieved May 5, 2003, from http://epaa.asu.edu/epaa/v10n12/

Wereschagin, M. (2007, September 11). Pittsburg study: Teachers key in affecting pupils' success. *Pittsburgh Tribune-Review.* Retrieved September 11, 2007, from http://www.ctlonline.org/ESEA/newsletter.html#Best%20Practices

Werner, E., & Smith, R. (1992). *Overcoming the odds: High-risk children from birth to adulthood.* New York: Cornell University Press.

Williams, B. (1996). *Closing the achievement gap: A vision for changing beliefs and practices.* Alexandria, VA: ASCD.

Williams, B. (2003). *Closing the achievement gap: A vision for changing beliefs and practices* (2nd ed.). Alexandria, VA: ASCD.

Winerip, M. (2007). In gaps at school, weighing family life. ASCD Newsbrief. Retrieved December 9, 2007, from http://www.smartbrief.com/news/ascd/search.jsp?searchTerm=in+gaps+at+school%2C+weighing+family+life&search.x=40&search.y=12&search=search+news

Zeichner, K. (2003). Pedagogy, knowledge, and teacher preparation. In B. Williams (Ed.), *Closing the achievement gap: A vision for changing beliefs and practices* (2nd ed., pp. 99–114). Alexandria, VA: ASCD.

Index

CORWIN

A SAGE Company

The Corwin logo—a raven striding across an open book—represents the union of courage and learning. Corwin is committed to improving education for all learners by publishing books and other professional development resources for those serving the field of PreK–12 education. By providing practical, hands-on materials, Corwin continues to carry out the promise of its motto: **"Helping Educators Do Their Work Better."**